FEDERAL WRITERS' PROJECT

MINNEAPOLIS
The Story of a City

AMS PRESS
NEW YORK

MINNEAPOLIS
The Story of a City

COMPILED BY WORKERS OF THE WRITERS'
PROGRAM OF THE WORK PROJECTS ADMIN-
ISTRATION IN THE STATE OF MINNESOTA

OFFICIAL SPONSOR, MINNESOTA DEPARTMENT OF EDUCATION
CO-SPONSOR, MINNEAPOLIS BOARD OF EDUCATION

1 9 4 0

Library of Congress Cataloging in Publication Data

Writers' Program. Minnesota.
Minneapolis.

Reprint of the 1940 ed.
At head of half title: Federal Writers' Project.
"Official sponsor: Minnesota Department of Education."
Bibliography: p.
1. Minneapolis—History. 2. Fort Snelling, Minn.—
History. I. Federal Writers' Project.
F614.M557W74   1976   977.6'579   73-3629
ISBN 0-404-57930-2

Reprinted from an original copy in the collections
of the Newark Public Library

From the edition of 1940, Minneapolis
First AMS edition published in 1976
Manufactured in the United States of America

AMS PRESS, INC.
NEW YORK, N. Y. 10003

Foreword

In the modern progress of a large city, the stirring and significant events of its earlier growth often are little heard of or are quickly forgotten by the very people who benefit most from the hard-won achievements of its pioneers.

A comprehensive history such as *Minneapolis: The Story of a City*, made easily available to the people of the community, becomes a valuable contribution to their knowledge, a permanent record of the community's origin and development. The book's account of obstacles overcome, of continuous growth from year to year, provides a stimulus for still further growth and improvement.

To people living elsewhere who may see this book, it will, I believe, be an invitation to consider Minneapolis as a good place in which to live, or an interesting place to visit—a point of some importance in consideration of Minneapolis' present active effort to attract new residents, new business, and more vacation visitors.

The casual reader of this book, even though he enjoy and profit by its contents, scarcely will understand the vast amount of careful study and research, the thought and planning given to its contents and arrangement, and the long hours of writing, editing and revision which made it the well done volume that it is.

The Minnesota Writers' Project of the Work Projects Administration is to be complimented on its creation and production of *Minneapolis: The Story of a City*. The Minneapolis Board of Education and the Minneapolis Public Schools personnel are glad to have been able to co-operate in this educational project.

CARROLL R. REED,
Superintendent of the
Minneapolis Public Schools.

Preface

In presenting this highlighted history of century-old Minneapolis, the Minnesota Writers' Project feels that it may be offering the reader something a modest bit out of the ordinary. As history itself, the work is obviously unpretentious. It is not possible in a hundred pages to treat very exhaustively the story of a hundred years in the life of a large city.

Yet it is suggested that the discerning reader may discover, even in this small volume, a definite contribution to the writing of history in the Northwest. The primary framework upon which it has been built is a certain Project file we call the Minnesota Newspaper Annals. We like to feel that this book speaks eloquently, on page after page, of the value of the Annals, not merely in the writing of this particular work, nor even of all the other Project books to follow, but in the writing of Minnesota history for many, many years to come. Leading librarians of the state, having sensed its richness as a source of historical material, are already seeking to obtain custody of our Annals file at the time when it shall have served its Project purposes.

The Minnesota Newspaper Annals are made up of many thousands of items upon a wide variety of subjects, culled by our research workers from the files of early Minnesota newspapers. These have been copied word for word from the fragile, yellowed pages of old newspaper volumes, and classified and filed in our office under a comprehensive index. A few years from now, the original sources may in many cases have crumbled away or become illegible; in the form to which we have now reduced them, these selected items can be bound and preserved for perhaps another hundred years.

Liberal quotations from contemporary comment can be used to enliven almost any history text; they tend to breathe vitality into pages which might otherwise be dry and lifeless. The things an editor had to say about his own times may recreate the atmosphere of a given period much more effectively than page upon page of hearsay description. It is in recognition of this principle that we have drawn so freely upon Annals material in compiling *Minneapolis: The Story of a City*.

In acknowledging our debt to those who have had a hand in the building of this book, we therefore bow first to Miss Ethel Hepburn, the former Project member who had a principal part in organizing and promoting the Minnesota Newspaper Annals, and to Mr. Harlan R. Crippen, who in the writing of the manuscript has so neatly demonstrated the usefulness of these Annals as historical building material.

We are also grateful, of course, to a good many others: to Mr. Carl Vitz, librarian of the Minneapolis Public Library, and his staff, and especially to Miss Ruth Thompson, in charge of the Minneapolis Collection, for unfailing courtesy and helpfulness in the selection of pictures;

To Dr. Arthur J. Larsen, superintendent of the Minnesota Historical Society, and library staff, and in particular to Dr. Grace Lee Nute, curator of manuscripts, Mr. Willoughby Babcock, curator, and Mrs. Louise Blad, assistant curator of the museum, for their assistance in preparation of the manuscript and selection of pictures;

To Mr. Clement Haupers, regional supervisor of the WPA Art Program and state supervisor of the Minnesota WPA Art Project, to Mr. Leroy Turner, assistant state supervisor and staff;

To Mr. Alexis Caswell, secretary and business manager, Manufacturers' Association of Minneapolis, Inc., for useful information graciously given;

To Mr. Ben Ferriss, publicity director of the Minneapolis Civic and Commerce Association, for permission to reproduce the skyline photograph of Minneapolis; to Mr. Julius Weitzner of New York City, by whose kind permission we were able to reproduce Seth Eastman's painting of Fort Snelling; and to Harper and Brothers, New York City, for allowing us to use the picture of the Republican convention of 1892;

To Mr. Lee Grove, former assistant Project supervisor, who edited the manuscript;

Finally and especially, to Mr. Carroll R. Reed, superintendent of schools, Minneapolis Board of Education, whose unflagging interest and helpfulness far exceeded any obligations that might have been his as representative of the co-sponsor of this book.

To these and many others who have helped, our sincere thanks. May they all feel that *Minneapolis: The Story of a City* is a creditable product of the joint efforts of all of us.

THE MINNESOTA WPA WRITERS' PROJECT
Roscoe Macy, State Supervisor

CONTENTS

	PAGE
FOREWORD	3
PREFACE	4
THIS NEW WORLD	9
POWER AND AUTHORITY	12
THEY CAME FROM NEW ENGLAND	28
FROM THESE WILDERNESSES	43
MIGHTY KINGDOMS WILL EMERGE	61
ILLUSTRATIONS	78-82
NOTES ON ILLUSTRATIONS	83
SUGGESTED READING AND BIBLIOGRAPHY	85
INDEX	89

Cover by the Minnesota WPA Art Project

This New World
Early Exploration

> "To what power or authority this new world will become dependent after it has arisen from its present uncultivated state, time alone can discover. . . . There is no doubt that at some future period, mighty kingdoms will emerge from these wildernesses, and stately palaces and solemn temples, with gilded spires reaching the skies, supplant the Indian huts . . ."

Thus wrote Jonathan Carver in the autumn of 1766 after viewing the juncture of the "large, fair river," Wadapaw Menesotor, or Minnesota, with the mighty Mississippi.

This far-seeing New Englander was not the first white man to visit the spot or the region. As far back as 1635, Jean Nicolet led the French advance into the unknown Northwest; in 1658 and 1659 Radisson and Groseilliers brought back to Canada the first canoe-loads of furs from this region, and by 1660 they are credited in some quarters with having reached the future territory of Minnesota. In 1680 Michael Accault, Antoine Auguelle and Father Hennepin ascended the Mississippi, the first white men to pass near the present site of Fort Snelling and Minneapolis. Pierre Charles Le Sueur came up the Mississippi from Louisiana, reaching the mouth of the Minnesota River on the 19th of September, 1700. As a result of these voyages, Montreal, the center of French trading, was alive with stories of the vastness and wealth of the region, and French fur traders came more and more often through the uncharted woods and valleys. They were drawn by the promise of easy wealth—hides, furs and minerals. And it was easy wealth—beaver skins for a few gaudy trinkets, great piles of furs for a cheap rifle, almost anything for whiskey. They made no attempt to colonize, however, and because of this, even though they wielded some influence over the Indians, their hold on the territory was in reality weak.

Jonathan Carver was the first to visualize the vast possibilities for settlement. He had been brought up in the New England tradition which followed exploration with colonization, by clearing the forests and creating farms. And farms were to be the real conquerors of the northwest wilderness, though many years were to pass before the young American republic could do anything to aid in that conquest.

By the beginning of the 19th century, the nation was beginning to be curious about the vast expanse that stretched westward, and explorers were penetrating the wilderness. With the Louisiana Purchase in 1803 it became a matter of sovereignty as well as trade, and Jefferson succeeded in getting Congress to sponsor two bold attempts to know the western lands. Two great expeditions were sent out into the unknown. Lewis and Clark were assigned to explore the Missouri, and twenty-six-year-old Lieutenant Zebulon Pike was despatched with a company of twenty men up the Mississippi.

Pike's instructions read, "You will be pleased to obtain permission from the Indians who claim the ground, for the erection of military posts and trading houses, at the mouth of the river St. Pierre." (Later the Minnesota River.)

Lieutenant Pike left St. Louis in August, 1805. Under the shadow of towering bluffs, the little company proceeded northward up the great river. They arrived at the junction of the Minnesota with the Mississippi on the 21st of September. They put ashore on a small island, now named Pike's Island in the young officer's honor.

With Pike's arrival, the history of the white man's conquest of Minnesota began. For the first time, he raised the American flag in this wilderness, and immediately set about securing the position as a permanent outpost of his government. The site chosen was atop a high, white cliff commanding the junction of the two rivers. Its strategic value was apparent at once to Pike as a military man.

Two days later, at the mouth of the Minnesota, a treaty was signed with the Sioux, which ceded to the United States rights to "nine miles square at the mouth of the river St. Croix, also, from below the confluence of the Mississippi and St. Peter's [Minnesota], up the Mississippi, to include the Falls of St. Anthony, extending nine miles on each side of the river." With magnificent and prophetic finality, Article I of the treaty provided "That the Sioux nation grants to the United States, the full sovereignty and power over said districts, forever, without any let or hindrance whatsoever." As soon as the treaty was signed Pike distributed two hundred dollars worth of merchandise and 60 gallons of whiskey, promise of which had evidently made the Sioux decision easier.

The young officer was much impressed with the country and determined to see more of it. However, his further exploration was beset with disaster—sledges fell through the ice, bitterly needed supplies were lost, fire destroyed a tent, his men suffered with frozen feet and fingers. Outside of gaining some slight knowledge of the headwaters of the Mississippi, little was accomplished. The Americans shot down the Union Jack from the Leech Lake Post of the Northwest Company, but in spite of this, British traders continued their activities.

Pike returned to St. Louis the following April. He had succeeded in his most important mission. There was some question of the legality of his treaty with the Sioux, but it was much too favorable to be thrown away. Three years later, April 16, 1808, it was ratified by the U. S. Senate. In deference to possible feeling among the Indians, the Senate agreed to pay them two thousand dollars worth of goods in addition to those which Pike had distributed.

By this time the young republic was torn with political strife, and then the War of 1812 began. Extension of the western frontier had to be postponed; it was 1817 before it was resumed.

In that year Major Stephen H. Long, of the corps of the Topographical Engineers, was sent to examine the land covered by Pike's treaty with the Sioux. He made a careful survey and returned a recommendation to the War Department. He had settled on the point of convergence of the two rivers, giving as his reasons: "A military work of considerable magnitude might be constructed on the point, and might be rendered sufficiently secure... The work on the point would be necessary to control the navigation of the two rivers."

The government was now ready to act. Rumors that a British colony had been founded on the borders of the United States and that British traders were extending operations in the area, speeded the matter. Major Thomas Forsyth was sent out to distribute among the Indians the amount of goods set by the Senate when Pike's treaty had been ratified. This payment had been conveniently overlooked pending a definite decision.

Power and Authority
The Rise of Fort Snelling

Early in February 1819, United States troops stationed at Prairie du Chien, Wisconsin, under Colonel Henry Leavenworth, were sent out to establish a post at the site selected by Major Long. Major Forsyth joined Leavenworth at Prairie du Chien, and on August 8th the expedition, with 118 men of the Fifth Regiment of Infantry, many of them veterans of the War of 1812, made its way up the Mississippi. Forsyth arrived at the mouth of the Minnesota on August 24, 1819, and Leavenworth arrived with the troops the next day. After surveying the area Leavenworth decided on a spot on the right bank of the Minnesota, just above the river's mouth, where Mendota now stands, and ordered it cleared. In September, 120 additional recruits arrived, and log cabins and a rude stockade were erected. With the usual optimism of the frontier, it was christened "Cantonment New Hope."

The winter which followed at New Hope was heartbreaking. A keelboat of supplies was held down-river by ice, and the provisions on hand were inadequate and of poor quality. Scurvy broke out and raged through the tiny settlement. It was believed that the disease was due to barrels of pork, from which the brine had been drawn to facilitate delivery, and which later were refilled with river water. Each of the crowded little snow-locked cabins had its share of misery, and by spring the lonely outpost had more than forty new graves.*

Leavenworth was convinced that the location of New Hope was unhealthy, and he determined to seek a better place. The men were also impatient to leave the settlement where they had spent such a horrible winter, especially when in May the swollen river, freed of ice, threatened to flood New Hope. The garrison was ordered to break camp and move to the other side of the river, about a mile from the place where the Fort now stands. This new cantonment they named "Camp Coldwater," because of the icy spring that bubbled near their shelters. Coldwater was not meant to be permanent. As a permanent site Leavenworth chose a spot on the first rise, about 300 yards west of the present Fort.

---

* Baker, General James, Address at Fort Snelling in the Celebration of the Centennial Anniversary of the Treaty of Pike With the Sioux, *Minnesota Historical Collections*, Vol. 12, Page 239. Folwell says (*History of Minnesota*, Vol. 1, Page 138) that the number of victims is a matter of dispute. Charlotte Van Cleve (*Three Score Years and Ten*, Page 19) gives the definite figure of forty while other estimates are higher.

During the summer the Camp was visited by an exploring party from the Yellowstone expedition at Camp Missouri, near the present city of Omaha. These men were engaged in trying to map an overland route which would connect the two small outposts. The welcome guests were "most kindly and hospitably received and entertained by Col. L. and his Lady."

Early that spring, soldiers had been set to cultivating about ninety acres of bottom and prairie land. Nathan Clark, Commissary of the Fort, had been instructed by General Gibson, Commissary General of Subsistence, to investigate the possibility of wheat raising there. By midsummer, when Governor Cass of Wisconsin visited the Camp with his exploring party, he was given green corn, peas, beans, cucumbers, beets, radishes and lettuce from the Post garden. Wheat was already ripe and there was a good stand of Indian corn and potatoes. This experiment was one of the first tests of the fertility of the soil, and it opened a new vista toward the development of the region. In the years following, the garrison acreage increased and extensive farming operations were carried on.

The summer of 1820 also brought to the Fort Lieutenant Lawrence Taliaferro, who had been appointed by President Monroe as Indian Agent for the area. Taliaferro was to play a most important role in the activities of the Fort for many years to come. This young Virginian had two main aims in his work among the Indians, and was impatient and intolerant of anything which might conflict with his purposes. First, he wished to prevent the recurring outbreaks of hostilities among the tribes; and secondly, he hoped to put into effect his plan for establishing the Indians in self-sustaining agricultural colonies.

The new agent immediately clashed with Leavenworth. On more than one occasion he predicted that the Colonel's gifts of whiskey to the Indians would cause trouble. His prediction was borne out when Chief Mahgossau, or White Buzzard, was stabbed by another Indian in an attempt to get whiskey which Leavenworth had given the chief.

In August 1820, Leavenworth was relieved of his duties at the outpost and replaced by Colonel Josiah Snelling. The morale of the Post, considerably impaired during the latter part of Leavenworth's regime, improved at once under the new commandant, who infused everyone with new life and energy. Plans for the Fort were altered and improved. The site finally chosen for its erection was a more advantageous spot at the high point of the bluff. An energetic, irascible soldier, Snelling set about giving the Fort permanence. The cornerstone of Fort St. Anthony, as it was then known, was laid on September 10, 1820, with ceremony. "The band played, songs were sung and whiskey issued," and the Fort began to rise.

Soon after taking up residence at the frontier outpost, Mrs. Josiah

Snelling gave birth to a baby daughter, Elizabeth, the first white child to be born in Minnesota. The Fort, a short time before the Snellings' arrival, had also been the scene of the first white marriage in Minnesota, that of Captain Gooding's daughter, Amelia, to Lieutenant Platt Rogers Green of the Fifth Infantry. The ceremony was performed by Colonel Leavenworth.

Because the new buildings were not yet ready for occupancy, the troops spent the winter of 1820-21 in the old cantonment at New Hope.

To provide the lumber needed for building, it was decided to erect a sawmill at the Falls of St. Anthony. This was put up in 1821 and equipped with a "muley saw," a quick-acting upright saw. Men had been sent up the Rum River to cut timber, and in the spring the logs came down, but as the mill was not yet completed, most of the lumber had to be cut out by whip saws. This rough lumber was then carted by team to the site of the new Fort.

Stone was cut from the Trenton limestone which forms the upper part of the Mississippi bluffs between the Fort and the Falls of St. Anthony. This was the first quarrying in Minnesota.

The soldiers working on the buildings were given an additional fifteen cents per day, and Snelling drove them hard. But even with Snelling to hasten construction, the Fort was not ready to be occupied until late in 1821, and was not completed, with the Indian Council House and the Round Tower, until much later.

The year 1821 brought the first of the hundreds of discouraged refugees that were to come from the drouth-stricken and grasshopper-plagued Selkirk colony. Alexis Bailly, fur trader at Mendota, brought five Swiss families with him on his return from the Red River Valley. They were permitted to settle as "squatters" near the Fort and were aided with provisions by Colonel Snelling. Many of them found useful employment around the garrison. They were the first agriculturists to settle in Minnesota. In 1823, thirteen more families came, but these continued southward, seeking a warmer, more congenial climate. Cold, drouth, a grasshopper plague, and finally the Red River flood of 1826, drove more and more colonists away from the Selkirk settlement. In all, 248 refugees came to the Fort; some of them traveled onward, but a number remained.

In 1823, after the garrison was completely moved into the new Fort, a post school was established. A building near the main entrance, in which the offices of the commandant, paymaster, quartermaster and commissary were located, was also used as the schoolhouse. John Marsh was employed as tutor at an annual salary of $75; this income he supplemented by carrying the mail between the Fort and Prairie du Chien for an additional $40 a year. The school was small and the children of most varied ages. There were the four Snelling children, Henry, Josiah, Mary and William Joseph; Charlotte and Malcolm Clark; James W. Hamilton; and John and Andrew Tully. Charlotte Clark, the baby of the class, was only four years old. William Joseph Snelling could hardly be called a child, since he was twenty and had probably seen more of life than the teacher.

This was education under the most trying circumstances, and Marsh only lasted two years at the job. One of his pupils later commented that "He was considered very competent for his work but was a violent tempered man and only maintained his position a few years." After Marsh left, most of the teaching was done by the officers' wives. French, still much needed on this part of the frontier, was taught by Simon, formerly an officer under Napoleon Bonaparte.

In May 1823, the *Virginia*, the first steamboat to appear at the Fort, was welcomed with booming cannon. The Indians were astonished and dismayed at the "monster of the waters," a new evidence of the mighty power of the white man. When the "fire-boat" blew off steam they fled to hiding places in terror. The citizens of the garrison settlement, however, were overjoyed at this promise of contact with the outside world. The arrival of the *Virginia* opened a new era for Minnesota. Previously it had been believed that the river was not navigable by steamboat north of St. Louis, and there was "great speculation as to whether the steamboat *(Virginia)* would ever return." By 1826 fifteen steamboats had visited the Fort.

Snelling's plans for the Fort were completed before the arrival of the *Virginia*. Like a medieval castle, the ponderous Round Tower of solid native stone frowned down upon the river from its hundred foot bluff. Twenty rifle slits allowed firing in any direction. The first row of barracks was of hewn pine, other buildings were of stone, and all were enclosed within a high stone wall. Snelling knew that the Fort could resist any form of attack known at the time. He felt it was a worthy symbol of the government he was pledged to extend and uphold in the wilderness.

Late in that year Mrs. Snelling and Mrs. Clark, wife of a lieutenant, started the first Sunday school in the basement of the colonel's quarters. Soldiers and their wives attended, and it was recorded that it was "productive of much good." A Bible school for officers and their wives aroused such interest that it "furnished topics of conversation for the week."

The experiment in wheat growing proved successful, and the commissary was ordered to make use of it to supply part of the flour needed for the garrison. A grist mill was built near the sawmill at the Falls, and fittings for it—one pair of buhr mill stones, 337 pounds of plaster of paris and two dozen sickles—were sent from St. Louis. The first flour-making could hardly be called a success, for the bread produced from it was black and bitter. When it was issued the troops brought it with them to the parade grounds and threw it on the ground before Colonel Snelling. The flour having proved unfit for use, there was a serious shortage of supplies the following winter. Of all the commodities, it seemed there was a sufficiency only of whiskey! Despite the difficulty, flour milling had begun—and the small beginning was prophetic of the great mills that were later to rise on the same site.

The next spring brought General Winfield Scott to the Fort for the first official inspection. He was greatly impressed by the efficiency and dispatch with which his "old comrade," Snelling, had transformed the rude, straggling outpost of a few years before into a handsome, well-planned Fort, and on his return to Washington he suggested that the post be re-named in Snelling's honor. An order to that effect was issued by the War Department, and Fort St. Anthony became Fort Snelling.

The War Department intended the Fort as a center of Indian activities, and a base for extending dominion throughout the entire Northwest. At the time of its establishment and for years after, Fort Snelling was the extreme northwestern point occupied securely by white men. By 1890 there was a population of ten million beyond that point, so well had it accomplished its purpose. The troops stationed there performed every sort of frontier duty. At times, detachments from the garrison traveled hundreds of miles to aid threatened posts and to protect settlers.

Fort Snelling itself was never the scene of serious trouble with the Indians, although there were many minor disturbances. It was Major Taliaferro's idea that tribal differences among the Indians might be settled by efforts to bring about understanding between rivals. However, experiments in this direction were not very successful.

In 1820 Cass had secured at the Fort the signature of Sioux and Chippewa to a treaty of peace. Three years later Taliaferro tried it again. But before the delegations were outside the Government Reserve, troops had to be called out to avert a bloody fracas. A conclusive peace was signed with impressive ceremony at a "grand conference" at Prairie du Chien in 1825. A year had not passed before Sioux warriors attacked a band of Chippewa within a short distance of Taliaferro's office. In 1827 there was more serious trouble, this also after a peace pipe had been smoked by Chippewa and Sioux. On the next evening Sioux warriors fired on unsuspecting Chippewa, killing two and wounding many at the very gates of the Fort. Snelling captured four Sioux and turned them over to the Chippewa for punishment according to the savage code. They were given thirty yards start and told to run for their lives. Shots quickly cut short the race, after which the bodies of the Sioux were scalped and mangled with knives.

Soon it was revealed that two of the four had been innocent, and open hostilities between Sioux and whites were barely averted. Criticism of Snelling's action was widespread, and the Sioux began a secret, silent war against the soldiers. Several of these disappeared, and were considered deserters until their bodies were discovered.

Explorers used the Fort as a base for their operations into the west and north. In July 1823, an expedition under Major Stephen Long reached Snelling on its way to the Red River and the Canadian border. The staff of the expedition included a zoologist, a geologist and a landscape painter. Giacomo Beltrami, an Italian exile, for whom Beltrami County was later named, had arrived at the Fort shortly before, and received permission to accompany Long's party to Pembina. Major Taliaferro, much impressed with the talented Italian, presented Beltrami with his "noble steed Cadmus" and provisions for the journey. Beltrami returned on September 15th, without Cadmus, but welcome none the less.

Meanwhile, under the protection of the Fort, Mendota, the former cantonment New Hope, had become a fur trading post for the entire region west and north to the Canadian boundary. Restriction of the fur trade to American citizens had given virtual monopoly to the American Fur Company of John Jacob Astor. In 1834 a branch of that important house was established in Mendota, and Henry H. Sibley took over the managership. Mendota's future seemed assured. Indians, fur traders, travelers who were surveying the prospects of trade and future settlement in the "Suland," as land west of the Mississippi was later known, made of Mendota a thriving community. Great trains of creaking Red River carts, rough two-wheeled affairs, made entirely of wood and drawn by oxen, came regularly from Pembina, loaded with furs and escorted by *Bois Brules* (burnt woods), or mixed bloods, attired in barbaric and colorful costumes. Here, also, most of the Sioux and Chippewa trading was transacted. But its hopes of becoming a great city were doomed, for when in 1849 the Astor Company moved to a more favorable location in St. Paul, Mendota began to wane.

In the five years after the completion of the Fort, Josiah Snelling ruled with a firm hand, although he chafed under the monotonous routine of fort life. Once the job of building the Fort was over, there were few outlets for a man who loved action, and these few were not very exciting. He often turned to the whiskey bottle for solace. In 1827 the Indians near Prairie du Chien killed several whites and fired on supply boats bound for Snelling. The Colonel took a company down the river to quell the uprising, but after an absence of six weeks the party returned without having fired a gun.

The men, too, were restive under the imposed duties of farming and mowing hay; they expressed themselves as wanting "shooting and stabbing." Some were driven to the extreme of deserting, although it was highly dangerous. In 1823 there were three deserters, in 1824 twenty-two and by 1825 there were twenty-nine. Indians were paid a reward of twenty dollars for each deserter they brought back. It was sometimes said that the walls of the Fort were "rather erected to keep the garrison in, than the enemy out." Close confinement in winter and the restricted social life within the Fort caused further tension.

Discipline necessarily grew more and more severe. Two hundred lashes on the naked back of an erring soldier was a punishment common to the army in that time. By 1826 dissension among the officers became an important problem. Snelling was challenged to a duel but refused to accept, whereupon his son, William Joseph, accepted in his place, lost a finger and was court-martialed. In the investigation that followed William insulted an officer and another duel was fought, but this time only the clothing of the participants suffered damage. Snelling himself accepted a duel with a "bad man," Lieutenant Baxby, "to be fought at four paces with pistols . . . firing to continue until one of the parties is killed or disabled." There is, however, no record of this duel being fought. Yet notwithstanding his exacting and arbitrary conduct of military affairs, Snelling was not a martinet, and his family and friends knew him as a kindly and considerate man. Taliaferro had found in him a most dependable support for his Indian policies.

On October 2, 1827, Snelling embarked on the steamer *Josephine*, with his wife, three children and "female servant Olympia," to take up his new appointment at Jefferson Barracks, near St. Louis. As the boat passed down the river he took a last look at the Fort he had built, now mellowed somewhat, not quite so stark and new, set in the golden autumn. A year later at the age of forty-six, he died.

Life at the Fort grew ever more uneventful as the land became settled; the garrison was more and more occupied with the unexciting, unchronicled, constructive work of peace. Routine was broken only by building, by births, and an occasional quiet death. Visitors were frequent, usually on their way to more distant places, but always enlivening the Fort and providing weeks of conversation and speculation. Missionaries held prayer meetings, teachers brought news of happenings in the outside world and explorers spiced the evenings with tales, often gruesome and adventurous.

Holidays were celebrated, not elaborately but as limited opportunities would allow. An interesting detail of early life at the Fort is given in the record of Christmas celebrations, contained in Taliaferro's journal, "Christmas Day: Serenade this morning at 3 oclk by the musicians." At daylight there were "3 Rounds by the French Inhabitants of the Post with the usual complements [sic] of the Season . . . Indians both men & women called at 11 oclk . . . in considerable numbers to see & shake hands & express the feelings of the day . . . The feelings of the heart were expressed before I was aware by a few Yellow Kisses—& amusing scene." The Indians had been trained in their Christmas and New Year's observances by the French Canadians and called the holidays "Kissing days." It grew to be an annual ordeal for the Indian Agent. Years later he complained that there were "many & old as well as young women" who participated.

After 1832 steamships arrived more regularly at the Fort. Almost every boat brought excursionists and visitors, for the trip was "considered more wonderful in those days than would be a trip to the Hawaiian Islands now," and distinguished men and women from all over the world came to view its promised wonders.

In the summer of 1832 Major Taliaferro brought his wife to the Fort. She was a "very handsome woman" and took an immediate part in the social life of the garrison.

At about this time punishment for wayward soldiers was changed from flogging to imprisonment in the "Black Hole," cut off from all light, on a diet of bread and water. An Irishman by the name of Kelley, who persisted in replying to orders "I'll be damned if I do," was placed here, without the bread and water, for three days. He stubbornly refused to recant, and the commandant was wondering how to account for his anticipated death when the soldier surrendered. After that experience his behavior was satisfactory.

Samuel and Gideon Pond arrived at the Fort on the steamboat *Warrior* in May 1834. The brothers had no permit to enter the country, but had been "constrained by the love of Christ," and without conferring with anyone had set out to "improve the Sioux." Major John Bliss held a hearing to determine whether to allow the Ponds to stay. Taliaferro desired them to, and his view finally prevailed. The Agent had established an Indian agricultural colony, Eatonville, near Lake Calhoun, and saw in the Pond brothers worthy and able assistants. The colony, which had begun with 12 Indians, had increased to 125 by 1832. They had planted a good deal of corn, but did not know how to plow. The Indian village at Kaposia, near the Fort, had also entered a request for plowing.

Samuel Pond volunteered to go to Kaposia, and the tall sinewy Presbyterian, leading a yoke of oxen, set out to improve the lot of the Sioux in a very practical way by teaching them to plow. At first his charges refused to touch the implement, but he persevered until they began to experiment for themselves. Gideon was sent to instruct the Sioux at Eatonville in tilling the soil. Both won the respect of the Indians and finally settled near Lake Calhoun where they built a two room cabin as a mission station and school. The unflinching devotion of these men to their self-appointed work won the admiration of both white and Indian.

Meanwhile, during the same year, the Reverend Thomas S. Williamson made a tour for the American Board of Foreign Missions, after which a missionary group was appointed to take up the work of God in Minnesota. They arrived at Fort Snelling May 16, 1835, under the leadership of the Reverend Mr. Williamson. Shortly after his arrival, Williamson married a young couple at the Fort, the daughter of Colonel Loomis to Lieutenant E. A. Ogden. This was the first marriage in Minnesota at which a clergyman officiated. Two weeks after Williamson, another group of missionaries also appointed by the American Board arrived at the Fort, under the leadership of the Reverend Jedediah D. Stevens.

Colonel Loomis, the commandant, a devout man, encouraged Williamson to organize a church. The missionary soon brought a committee together, and on June 14, 1835, services were held in the first organized Protestant church in the upper Mississippi Valley. Williamson chose as his text, "For ye were as sheep going astray, but are now returned to the Shepherd and Bishop of your souls." Samuel Pond became one of the elders of the new church. The First Presbyterian Church of Minneapolis is a continuation of that first organized worship.

George Catlin, famous painter of Indian life, was one of several prominent visitors to the Fort during the summer of 1835. Major Taliaferro informed the Indians that Catlin was a powerful medicine man and promised them that the cannon would be fired twenty-one times if they would entertain him on the Fourth of July with a game of lacrosse and an exhibition of tribal dances.

When the day came, hundreds of Indians appeared at the Fort in gala attire. They were presented with gifts by Catlin. Rival teams of Sioux and Chippewa played the rough, exciting game, those most skilled wearing white horse tails as a symbol of proficiency. The game was followed by the beggar's dance, the buffalo dance, the bear dance, the eagle dance and the dance of the braves. The latter—in which the golden bodies of the braves were adorned only with feather girdles—Catlin afterward described as "peculiarly beautiful and exciting to the feelings in the highest degree." In the evening before the Indians returned to their camps and villages, cannon boomed over the river, as Taliaferro had promised.

Joseph Nicolas Nicollet, a young Frenchman who had received War Department permission to explore in the region, arrived at the Fort in the summer of 1836, and was given a hearty welcome. He traveled throughout the north country, returning to the Fort on September 27th. A spell of cold weather led him to decide to spend the winter at the Post, and during this time he devoted himself to studying the Sioux and

Chippewa languages. He was a most welcome guest, for he was an accomplished violinist and spent many evenings playing, accompanied on the piano by Mrs. Taliaferro.

The whole garrison found diversion in amateur theatricals. The first presentation of which we have record was on October first, 1836, a performance of *Monsieur Tonson*, a popular farce, and *The Village Lawyer*. The entire Fort was ransacked for properties for these productions. Soldiers played all the characters, so those taking women's parts had to make "a generous sacrifice to art of . . . whiskers and moustaches." The appearance of these ungainly "women" caused much amusement. These first dramatic presentations in Minnesota were so successful that afterward the soldiers would "get up theatrical performances every fortnight or so."

During this period, Dr. John Emerson was stationed at the post. He had brought north with him a Negro slave, Dred Scott. Upon Dr. Emerson's death, his widow moved to St. Louis, in slave territory. Here, Scott, aided by wealthy and powerful sons of his previous owner, Peter Blow, sued for his freedom on the grounds that his residence at Fort Snelling, in territory where slavery was prohibited under the Missouri compromise, had made him a free man. The Supreme Court, when appealed to, declared the Missouri Compromise unconstitutional and thus precipitated the events leading to the Civil War.

On June 27, 1837, one of the more or less regular trains of Red River carts arrived at the Fort from the northern settlements. Among the travelers in the caravan was Peter Garrioch, a young Canadian school teacher, traveling east for further education. The Reverend J. D. Stevens of the Sioux Mission at Lake Harriet persuaded the young man to take care of the Mission until Stevens could journey to New York and return. Garrioch consented, and in the fall, on the last steamer, Stevens returned. The captain, fearing that the boat would be caught by ice, departed in a hurry, before Garrioch could get on board. Thus the young teacher found himself stranded at Fort Snelling for the winter, in need of a means of earning his living. He determined to open a school at Baker's Settlement, a small cluster of cabins around the trading house of Benjamin F. Baker, on the former site of Camp Coldwater.

This school opened on December first. Garrioch was not entirely satisfied with the results, for he wrote in his diary: "Opened my school on the heterogeneous system. The whole number of brats that attended for the purpose of being benefited by my notions, on my philosophical plan, amounted to thirty. This number is composed of English, French, Swiss, Cree, Chippewa, Sioux and Negro extraction. Such a composition and such a group of geniuses, I never saw before. May it never be my privilege to meet another. It staggered my gifts . . . to keep up with the brights.

I question whether an antiquarian of the most celebrated longevity ever lived . . . who could produce a specimen of such dolts and dunderheads as were clustered together in my school."

Another visitor to the Fort during the summer of 1837 was Mrs. Elizabeth S. Hamilton, the widow of Alexander Hamilton. The eighty-year-old woman had come west to visit a son in Wisconsin and had determined to see as much of the country as possible, including Fort Snelling. Her reception was probably the most elaborate ever given there up to that time.

Major Joseph Plympton, who took command in August 1837, at once interested himself in defining the limits of the military reservation and the number of settlers. It was found there were 82 white inhabitants in Baker's Settlement, and that these with others made up a total of 157 persons who had no connection with the garrison.

Also arriving in 1837 was Franklin Steele, later to play an important role in the affairs of the Fort. The next year he was appointed sutler of the Post by President Van Buren.

Captain Frederick Marryat was another visitor of the same year. The British novelist was not long welcome. He was presented with a gift by the Sioux, and in his speech of acceptance he advised the Indians that if there should ever be war again between Britain and the United States "you should not take part with the Americans." Taliaferro was informed of this and Marryat was advised that his stay in the Fort territory had ended.

The steamship *Ariel*, first boat to arrive at Fort Snelling in 1839, brought twenty barrels of whiskey. The next boat brought six barrels, all of it intended for the use of traders in the vicinity. The surgeon at the Fort complained to Washington, "There is a citizen named Brown" who is "actually building . . . within gunshot of the Fort, a very expensive whiskey shop." The surgeon's fears were more than justified, for drinking caused disturbances among both soldiers and Indians. On June 30th, after a visit to "Brown's Groggery," forty-seven of the soldiers spent the night in the guard house for drunkenness. Major Plympton determined to rid the Fort of the nuisance and called for the evacuation of all white settlers within twenty miles.

The settlers on the west side, who had originally squatted there with the tacit permission of the authorities, were thus innocent victims of this fight against the whiskey sellers. They did not obey the order and organized to protest to Congress. However, in May 1840, the garrison moved on the settlement, ejecting the people and their goods and unroofing the houses. The settlers sent a claim for damages to Congress, where it was promptly pigeonholed and forgotten.

The most important event of 1839 was the voluntary resignation of Indian Agent Taliaferro. His Indian agricultural colony had been brought to an end by Sioux and Chippewa hostilities and his work for the Indians seemed hopeless. He wrote that he knew then, "The time would come when all my efforts to do good would pass into oblivion and the nationality of the noble Sioux be completely destroyed." He, more perhaps than anyone else, had seemed a part of the Fort. Regiments came and departed, officers were transferred, but he had remained.

Early in Taliaferro's career, traders and politicians had found that he could not be bribed or frightened into conniving against the Indians, and this did not endear him to them. In 1830 he prevented the American Fur Company from collecting through the government on credits to the Indians, and afterwards was counted a dangerous enemy by that powerful corporation.

On September 9, 1839, a final humiliating event occurred which brought about his resignation. On that day a group of Sioux crossed to the east shore of the Mississippi and burned the grog shop of some whiskey traders. On October 5th Henry C. Menck, one of the whiskey sellers, having obtained an illegal appointment as a special deputy sheriff from Clayton County, Iowa, forced Taliaferro's door. He threw the Indian Agent, who was ill and in bed, to the floor, held him there, threatened him with a pistol and informed him that he was under arrest for burning the grog shop, and that sick or well he must go to Clayton Court House. First, though, Taliaferro was permitted to send the commandant a message informing him of his departure. The result was a foregone conclusion. Menck was promptly taken into custody and expelled from the area with scant ceremony, but Taliaferro also did not long remain.

Concerning his resignation, Taliaferro wrote in his journal: "I leave the whole nest this fall of Indians and traders . . . I am disgusted with the life of an Agent among such bad materials and bad management on the part of Congress—The Indian Office &c&c." As he said, the Indian Office was "bending a listening ear to the agents of the American Fur Company," and all his efforts to aid the Indians were brought to nothing.

Zachary Taylor, commandant of the Fort from 1828 to 1829, and later President of the United States, had already testified that the American Fur Company was "the greatest set of scoundrels the world ever knew." This was a strong statement but the Indian Agent probably shared Taylor's opinion. Taliaferro's honesty and pride revolted at seeing his work defeated by that Company. He wrote, "I have the Sad Consolation of leaving . . . the public service as poor as when I first entered it . . . the only evidence of my integrity."

An important arrival of 1839 was the Reverend Ezekiel Gilbert Gear, who was chaplain of the post for the next nineteen years. He also acted as schoolmaster for the Fort school. He was the first resident Christian minister of a white community in Minnesota.

Captain Seth Eastman was appointed commandant of Fort Snelling in 1841 and held that post at intervals up to 1848. He was an artist, and left many drawings of the Fort and the surrounding country.

In 1843, the Protestant Episcopal Church sent Bishop Jackson Kemper to Fort Snelling to study the possibilities of work among the Indians. He saw much need for a mission among the Chippewa, and urged its immediate establishment. This mission, however, was not founded until 1852.

Settlement proceeded very slowly up until 1849, when the number garrisoned at the Fort was listed as two hundred. On April 9th of that year, news sped up the river that Minnesota had been made a Territory, and following this came settlers in swiftly increasing numbers. Until this time, St. Paul was known chiefly as an evil place that sold *Minne-wakan* (spirit water) to the Indians and traders. Now its population doubled and trebled because of the rumor that it was to be the territorial capital.

The present Reserve Township of Ramsey County was then included in the military reservation. A report was spread that the reservation area was to be reduced and that this portion of land would be thrown open to settlers. Overnight hundreds of shanties went up. When the invasion was reported to Colonel Loomis, he ordered a lieutenant with twenty mounted men to pull down every cabin and expel the would-be settlers.

News of the Sioux treaties of 1851 led settlers to invade the region west of the Mississippi river though it was still restricted territory. The Indian Agent remonstrated and labored to prevent this unlawful procedure, but neither the garrison nor public officials were zealous in the defense of Indian rights.

One of the settlers who came in October 1851, was Dr. Alfred Elisha Ames. With his family of six sons, Dr. Ames moved from Illinois to the Fort Snelling reservation, and became the first practicing physician in Minneapolis. Among his sons was Albert Alonzo Ames, then a boy of ten, who later became notorious in Minneapolis politics.

The forcible expulsion of the Selkirk refugees discouraged direct attempts to secure land in the military reserve. But pressure for settlement was almost irresistible, and in 1852 Congress reduced the original Fort reserve to the limits bounded by Minnehaha Creek and Lake Amelia (Nokomis). A bill was then entered to recognize the prior claims. Most of the squatters who had entered kept their plots of land but were afraid to build upon them. Not more than twelve dwellings had been erected before this year, though there were many claim shanties.

After the establishment of the Territory of Minnesota, the importance of Fort Snelling began to decline. The Chippewa were being subdued, and the Sioux had been removed to the Redwood area, so that there was agitation in some quarters for abandonment of the Fort and its sale to private citizens. There is reason to believe, however, that most of this agitation emanated from persons interested in the site as a source of speculative profits.

On June 6, 1857, under an act of Congress of March 3, 1835, authorizing the sale of certain military sites, Secretary of War John B. Floyd sold Fort Snelling reserve, with the exception of two small tracts, to Franklin Steele. The price was $90,000, with one third of the amount paid down and an agreement that the remainder should be paid in two equal annual sums. This sale was made without allowing others to bid, and a lively scandal resulted. It was believed that Steele was acting in behalf of a group of land speculators with good connections in Washington, and Secretary Floyd was later discredited and accused of "graft" in connection with the deal. One military man said later, with regard to it: "With a knowledge of this fact, we are now prepared to understand his [Floyd's] conduct in robbing the armories and arsenals of the country and turning their contents over to the southern people to be used against the government. . . . "

On July 19, 1858, the quartermaster relinquished the fort buildings and the first period in the history of old Fort Snelling was ended.

The year Franklin Steele took possession found business at a standstill, and real estate a drug on the market. He purchased a large herd of sheep and turned the grounds into a sheep ranch. In order to protect the herd at night they were driven inside the walls and permitted to occupy the houses. Eventually Steele's high hopes collapsed, and he defaulted on the next two payments. It seems that the sheep raising program also was abandoned, for in 1860 the Fort was the scene of the first Minnesota State Fair.

Then came the Civil War, and as no suitable quarters could be found in St. Paul for assembling troops, recruits were instructed to report to Fort Snelling. On April 29, 1861, the Stars and Stripes were again raised over the Fort, and mustering in began. The companies elected their own officers, who were afterward commissioned by the Governor. Minnesota had been asked for a regiment of 780 men—within two weeks she had nearly a thousand.

The First Minnesota Regiment was enlisted, but was without uniforms, ammunition or other equipment. The adjutant, lacking both money and authority, let contracts to local companies for needed supplies. The uniform provided was picturesque in the extreme, consisting of red flannel shirts, black trousers and "slouch" hats. This uniform was worn in the Battle of Bull Run where it proved a splendid target for rebel fire.

Food provisioning was also badly handled, and local contractors proved miserly. The men often refused to touch the inadequate and badly prepared meals; sarcastic and profane comment on the quality of the food was commonplace. These protests culminated in a virtual bread riot, after which matters were somewhat improved.

From 1861 to 1866 the Fort was occupied by troops. All Minnesota regiments and batteries in the Civil War were trained inside and around the walls of the Fort. Troops were kept there during the entire war, because of the Sioux Outbreak in 1862, and the fear that isolated communities might be subject to further attack.

In 1862 a young German army officer, Count Zeppelin, military attaché to the United States, was assigned to Fort Snelling and was quartered in the old Round Tower. It was while here that he first conceived his idea of lighter-than-air craft. He approached the Union military command with plans for an observation balloon. The idea was laughed down, but the young German was not so easily put off. He had the military tailor sew a canvas bag for him, and he filled it with as much illuminating gas as the old St. Paul Gas Company would allot to him. On a bright spring night in 1864 he made a thirty minute flight 300 feet above the tower. As a result of this flight his dream of future air travel took concrete form.

In 1864 two leaders of the Sioux uprising, Shakopee and Medicine Bottle, were arrested and brought to Fort Snelling for trial. They were tried in December, and sentenced to be hanged. Shakopee, a dignified old chief, who believed he had taken the only chance left to free his people, was stoic in his failure. A gallows was erected on a little knoll near the Fort and a great crowd gathered to witness the hanging. At the last moment, a railway whistle broke the hush that had settled upon the people. Shakopee raised his arm toward the sound and with quiet resignation said, "As the white man comes in, the Indian goes out." Then the trap fell.*

In 1868 Franklin Steele presented to the War Department a bill for

* Newson, Mary J., Memories of Fort Snelling in Civil War Days, *Minnesota History*, Vol. 15, No. 4, December 1934, Page 400. Also see An English Visitor of the Civil War Period, *Minnesota History*, Vol. 9, No. 4, December 1928, pp. 381-382.

Shakopee (Little Six) was hanged on November 11, 1865 (Folwell, W. W., *History of Minnesota*, Vol. 2, Page 293, 450). The first run over the Minnesota Valley Railroad, which is supposed to have been the whistle heard, took place on November 21, 1865 (St. Paul *Daily Pioneer*, November 22, 1865). These facts do not completely discount the incident. It is quite possible that work trains on trial runs would have sounded a whistle on the 11th.

$162,000 for rental on the reserve from 1861 to 1866. Secretary of War Edwin Stanton said, "That is one of Floyd's flyblown contracts and I will have nothing to do with it, unless I am directed to do so by Congress." A bill was presented to Congress settling the claim in Steele's favor. This bill was defeated through the efforts of Ignatius Donnelly, but at the next session it was passed. Further, the settlement reduced the reserve and gave Steele a large share of the land. About fifteen hundred acres were reserved for military purposes, and Fort Snelling has since remained a permanent training and army post.

Fort Snelling, like other frontier forts, was an institution not solely military in nature. Its function extended into many phases of pioneer life. It was the center of social activity and, in the very early days, of cultural life. Its history was not created with rifle and sword. To protect the work of axe and plow, to shelter the growth of a commonwealth, was Fort Snelling's honor and glory.

Its early inhabitants had great aspirations for the Fort. One writer said, "The original intention was to group the metropolis of the Upper Mississippi basin around this station [Fort Snelling] . . . for [with] the continual growth of these urban groups [St. Paul and Minneapolis] the Fort must become the natural center of the whole aggregate."

But as the years progressed the Fort was relegated to the background. The two great cities, which in their infancy were protected by it, outstripped it, surrounded it, and finally left it aside, almost forgotten. The tense days of the Civil War again, for a brief time, gave the Fort importance, but it was soon forgotten in the turbulent activity and industrial growth that followed. The dream of Jonathan Carver, the hopes of the settlers in the wilderness, were more than fulfilled in the magnificent cities arising on either side—but in their fulfillment the Fort, save for the routine activities of its garrison, has become little more than a memory of great beginnings.

They Came From New England
The Settlement of St. Anthony

By 1830-1840, the unknown Northwest was becoming known, and the settlers—farmers, lawyers, business men and artisans—were beginning to establish homes and communities in the new land.

It was inevitable that a great trade and business center should develop to serve the area. Men's views as to where this center should be were widely divergent, and they staked their fortunes and their future upon the outcome.

Almost certainly it would be on the Mississippi River, which, with its tributaries, provided easy transportation into the very heart of this land. St. Anthony's Falls, the most important break in transportation on the river, was a source of potential power, a base for manufacturing as well as commerce. Other factors favored its becoming the manufacturing and commercial center, such as the seemingly endless forests of pine to the north, and to the south and west the boundless wheat lands, corn lands and stock ranges that were steadily luring settlers to the region.

St. Anthony's Falls in the 1830's was widely known for its beauty; visitors to the nearby Fort had spread its fame far abroad. Long before these visitors came, the Indians had worshipped the Falls as the dwelling place of the Manitou, often throwing their most treasured possessions into the water, as an offering to the spirits dwelling there.

Now came ambitious men who saw in the Falls, not beauty, but power. The beauty they sought was civilization, wealth and trade, and the Falls would be a means of producing these things.

Not only was there power, but limitless forests were waiting to be transformed by that power into material for building the prosperous city of which they dreamed. So they moved to make that power their own. In 1836, before the Indian claim to the land was extinguished, Major Joseph Plympton, commandant of Fort Snelling, and Captain Martin Scott selected the land controlling the power site, and built a cabin as token of their prior claim. The following year Sergeant Nathaniel Carpenter staked out a claim next to Plympton's. It was against the law, since officers were not allowed to preempt land, but they could try, and hope.

However, another man had his eye on that land—one who knew the law and how to bide his time. This man was Franklin Steele, who visited the place in 1837, returned to his lumbering operations on the St. Croix, then traveled on to Washington. He came again to Fort Snelling, June 13, 1838, his plans apparently well laid. The next month the steamship *Palmyra* brought official news that the east river land had been opened and the Indian claim extinguished. That night, in secret, Steele with several other men crossed the river in the darkness, and built a makeshift cabin. Next morning, sensing something amiss, Captain Scott hurried to the claim and found Steele in possession. His protests were of no avail— Steele quoted the law against officers taking claims, and ordered Scott off the place. The officers, knowing they were beaten, withdrew without further dispute.

A permanent cabin was built on the claim, and Steele, because he was busy as sutler at the Fort, was forced to hire men to hold the claim for him. At this he was not as fortunate as he had been in establishing his claim. An old *voyageur*, LaGrue, was first placed in charge. While this man was away one day the cabin burned and his wife perished in the flames. LaGrue soon after disappeared into the wilderness. Another *voyageur*, Charles Landry, was then employed as caretaker. He was irresponsible and shiftless, and once when he was too long absent, Menck, an adventurer, jumped the claim.

There was no law by which Steele might evict him, but Menck was not particularly interested in land development, and proved amenable when Steele offered him several hundred dollars for vacating the claim. Afterward Steele installed Joseph Reachi, another Canadian *voyageur*, as caretaker, a man who brought with him his wife and seven children.

By 1845 a straggling population of less than fifty people was living in rude shacks along the eastern shore. Some were traders; others were holding claims, for themselves or for employers. Only one cabin, that occupied by Reachi, was shingled; the others were roofed with elm bark or sod. The opposite side of the river had one resident only: "Old Maloney," the man who took care of the government mill.

Of the actual settlers, the leading one was Pierre Bottineau, French-Indian trader and guide, who in 1844 had secured an interest in some claims, and the next year moved with his family and brother-in-law to the Falls. As trader for the American Fur Company, Bottineau had been active around the Falls since 1842, experimenting first with keelboats and then with flat boats, for navigating the upper river.

Steele in the meantime continued his efforts to dominate the development of the eastern shore. His purchase of the claims of Peter Quinn and his son-in-law Samuel J. Findley completed his control of the waterpower. By the close of the year 1845 the close friends, Bottineau and Steele, controlled all important land on the east side of the river. From his post as sutler at the Fort and through his connections at Washington, Steele was in a powerful position to aid and encourage development of the settlement.

To this end he approached eastern financiers in an attempt to secure capital for lumbering. This attempt was not at first successful. The men who were to furnish the money were not convinced that there was sufficient timber to make the venture profitable, and Steele himself could not speak with authority. He knew there was timber, but he did not know how much.

Early in 1847, Daniel Stanchfield, a hard-headed New Englander, came to the Fort and met Steele, who soon realized that here was the man for him. Stanchfield was first in a long succession of faithful, intelligent men whom the sutler chose for his aids. When Steele outlined his plans in detail Stanchfield was much impressed and undertook to go into the north country and make a report for the eastern financiers on the pine available. He found more potential wealth than either he or Steele had dared hope for.

Stanchfield's report convinced Caleb Cushing, Robert Rantoul and other eastern capitalists of the possibilities for investment. On July 10, 1847, nine-tenths of the water power rights were turned over to the financiers in return for the $10,000 needed for the construction of a dam and a sawmill, and to finance first operations. The money was not immediately forthcoming, but the promise was sufficient to start things moving.

Ard Godfrey was to come from Maine to supervise the building of the dam and sawmill; until he arrived Jacob Fisher of St. Croix supervised preliminary operations. Godfrey, with John McDonald and Ira Burroughs, reached the Falls in early autumn. There was little in the appearance of the place to encourage belief in its future. Near the Falls was Steele's cabin, then occupied by Luther Patch and his two daughters, Marion and Cora. A small field of corn grew nearby. To the north stood Pierre Bottineau's log house close to the shore, while near a ravine to the southward was Calvin Tuttle's shanty. These, with a few scattered cabins of French squatters, made up the entire settlement.

Men were sent north to bring down timber for building operations. Robert W. Cummings, Henry Angell, Captain John Tapper and William Dugas went up the Swan River while Daniel Stanchfield led another crew up the Rum River. Both expeditions suffered misfortune. The timber from the banks of the Swan was caught and frozen in at Pike Rapids. This timber was saved when the ice broke up in the spring but it was too late to help build the dam. The logs from the Rum River region were also frozen in and these were lost in the spring torrents.

Meanwhile Godfrey had noticed the beautiful groves of maple and elm on Nicollet and Hennepin Islands. To build the dam, these trees went down beneath the woodsmen's axes.

That winter brought more misfortune. A boat sank and was lost with all its supplies, including the hardware and tools that were necessary for building the mill and much needed homes. The winter was a severe one, and provisions were scarce. There were few women in the settlement, and the men had to do their own cooking and housekeeping, as well as their work in building and lumbering. The old government sawmill across the river, although still operating, was almost worn out, and its capacity at best was three or four hundred feet per day. Some lumber was hauled from St. Croix, but this was also insufficient for minimum needs. Some hardy pioneers actually hewed the wood for their homes out of hard tamarack, elm, and maple trees.

Stanchfield led another crew into the north, this time to bargain for a supply of timber with the Indians who held title to the woodland. After a conference, Chief Hole-in-the-Day asked that they be given five pair of blankets, some calico and broadcloth, fifty cents per tree and a pony in the spring. Stanchfield felt that this was an exhorbitant price but he finally agreed, with the provision that the cost of the presents should be taken out of the price paid for the trees. Lumbering then began in earnest.

A further misfortune now befell the settlement. Rantoul and Cushing failed to meet their payments, and Steele ran out of money. Since the settlement and its prosperity depended upon him, everyone felt the pinch of hardship. They kept on in spite of these difficulties, for the mill was their hope and upon it everything depended.

So far the growing community had been without the convenience of a store. Now Roswell P. Russell, who had worked for Steele at the Fort, brought over a small stock of goods from the sutler's supplies and displayed it in the front room of the house on Steele's claim which was occupied by Luther Patch and his two daughters. This house, at which Russell also boarded, was at what is now the corner of Second Ave. S. E. and Main Street. The entire stock of this first store was about one wagon load, and though later merchants might refer to it with contempt, it was greatly appreciated by the settlers. In the year following, a romance developed in this store and, on October 3, 1848, Miss Marion Patch became Mrs. R. P. Russell, the first marriage to be celebrated in the new village.

In the early days of the settlement, the only way to cross to the west side was by fording the river along a rock ledge at the foot of Nicollet Island. The current was swift at this point, however, and the building of the dam raised the water to a point where fording was no longer possible. Near Boom Island the river was more placid, and here canoe crossings could be made. An Indian woman, who earned her living by fishing, often added to her income by taking travelers across at this point in a canoe. Late in 1847 Steele financed the establishment of a regular ferry service. The equipment was primitive, consisting of a rope cable stretched from shore to shore along which moved a flat boat whose movable keel used the current as motive power. R. P. Russell took charge of the business of the line and Edgar Folsom was brought to the settlement to act as boatman.

One day a daughter of Reuben Bean struck the ferry cable with her canoe, which upset and plunged the girl into the river. She clung desperately to the cable until Folsom rescued her. In return for saving her life, the ferryman asked the maiden for her hand in marriage. One look at her rescuer was enough. "Put me back on the ferry rope," she pleaded. The story of his rejected proposal made Folsom the butt of so much ridicule that he soon left the settlement, and William Dugas took over the ferry.

Under the guidance of an experienced millwright, Ard Godfrey, work on the dam went steadily forward. In the summer of 1848, with the mill practically completed, Godfrey went back to Maine for his family. In September the mill opened, with two sash saws in operation. Difficulties began to ease up for the settlers. Some who had visited the place the preceding fall, and had been discouraged by the lack of lumber and tools with which to build, now returned to take up permanent residence. Among these was William R. Marshall, who was to play a prominent part in community affairs and who later became governor of the Territory.

One mill was not sufficient for the settlement's own needs, and St. Paul and other places were asking for lumber. Therefore plans were made and construction begun on a gang sawmill and two shingle mills, to be completed and working by the spring of 1849.

Before 1848 all of this land upon which the settlers were working, and upon which they were pinning their hopes, belonged to the Government. There had not been a survey, and no transfer of ownership could be legally recorded. This year the first Government sale took place, and the land was sold to the claimants at a dollar and twenty-five cents an acre. Steele found means of securing all the land which he considered valuable. Settlers had been hired to hold the best tracts for him; they bought it in this sale, with the provision that they would later transfer ownership to Steele. Other settlers sold their land to him as soon as their title was confirmed.

After the sale, Steele and Bottineau hired William R. Marshall to survey the townsite and lay it out in blocks and lots. A survey had been started earlier by S. P. Folsom but had never been completed. Marshall laid out the streets eighty feet wide, with the exception of Main Street, which was to be one hundred feet. Population of the settlement had reached 300, mostly men. Everyone expected many settlers the next spring. Most of the men had families coming, and everyone knew of friends "back east" who were preparing to make the journey. Word was spreading that Minnesota was to be made a territory. Platting the city had been the final preparatory step; St. Anthony waited expectantly.

The year that followed was one of startling growth. In the middle of April, 1849, the first boat arrived in St. Paul, bringing needed supplies, tools, and new settlers. Among the passengers was Mrs. Ard Godfrey, with her children. Godfrey had come back the previous fall and had built a home while his family had waited for navigation to open. In this house, two months after her arrival, Mrs. Godfrey gave birth to a daughter, Harriet Razada, the first white child of American lineage to be born in the settlement.

Every week brought newcomers. There was no hotel, aside from the rude boarding house kept for lumbermen, and the incoming settlers, if they were lucky, bunked with friends or acquaintances. Some had to sleep upon floors, others camped out until a cabin could be built.

Most of these new settlers were sturdy, thrifty New Englanders. Maine provided the largest number, many of them woodsmen from along the Penobscot. Others came from the hills of Vermont and New Hampshire. All trades and professions were represented and all worked first at lumbering. One, a doctor, often was called to his patients from the mill, arriving in sawdust-covered overalls. Soon, however, he found it possible to confine himself to his profession, for in that summer 40 children were born in the settlement.

Among other arrivals was Miss Electa Bachus, a young woman who had set out from her native Connecticut to be a missionary teacher among the Indians. At St. Anthony, however, she found herself among fellow New Englanders, who were not in need of missionaries, but whose children sorely needed instruction. Miss Bachus began a school soon after her arrival, in a small shanty, with only ten or twelve children in attendance. Before the end of summer the number had increased to forty and the room was overcrowded. A schoolhouse was erected in the fall, the first to be built except for the post school at Fort Snelling, within the present confines of Hennepin County.

Ard Godfrey was appointed postmaster in 1849, and the first post office was set up in the office of the lumber company. It consisted of an empty candlebox divided into compartments; people came in and took their own mail. The postmaster had to send to St. Paul for the mail as best he could; there was no regular transportation between the two places and no mail carrier. Captain John Rollins ran a passenger wagon to the larger city occasionally but this was not dependable. Regular stage coach service was not inaugurated until the following year.

In the spring William R. Marshall, in partnership with his brother Joseph, opened a store on Main Street to supply the growing demand for merchandise. This store was a front room in the Marshall brothers' residence, which had the distinction of being the first plastered building in the town. Marshall, ignoring Russell's makeshift stock of goods, called his the first store. There was sufficient business to attract other merchants also, and Russell went into partnership with Joel D. Cruttenden and opened a larger store in a new location. John G. Lennon opened a store for the American Fur Company, and Daniel Stanchfield also turned merchant. Stanchfield's store was the largest in the village at the time. Although business was good, cash was scarce. Some of the merchants accepted logs in payment and ran them down to the markets on the lower river. On this basis it took a year to get a cash return on merchandise sold.

Though money was scarce, everything seemed to prosper and grow. The mill began operating two new saws and the supply of lumber became somewhat more plentiful. To supply needed housing for travelers and new settlers, Anson Northup began construction of the St. Charles Hotel. Since the first deal with eastern capitalists had fallen through, cash for these new developments was badly needed. To meet this need Franklin Steele now sold a half interest in his holdings at the Falls to Arnold W. Taylor of Boston for $20,000. This proved to be a bad bargain, for Taylor was an irascible gentleman who could agree with no one and who seemed to care little whether the town developed or died. The result of his obstinacy was to retard the growth of the village, and two years later Steele was glad to buy back the interest for $25,000.

Development was so rapid that the settlement was soon possessed with ambitions far beyond its reach. When the first Territorial Legislature met in St. Paul in September, William Marshall, representing the interest of the thriving town, boldly demanded for St. Anthony the honor of being named Territorial capital, and vigorously opposed the passage of a bill locating it at St. Paul. The bill, of course, passed, but the fight was not wholly in vain, since later the Legislature decided to placate St. Anthony by locating the university there. During the winter 1850-1851 the citizens undertook to see that this valuable prize was not taken away from them, and, to prove that they took the matter seriously, raised $3,000 by popular subscription for the erection of a university building upon land donated by Franklin Steele. The first building, a crude wooden affair, was built near the mills facing Main Street and the Mississippi.

It was soon apparent, however, that this location was too close to the business and manufacturing section, and a new site, the present one, was secured.

The winter of 1849-1850 saw the beginning of social life in the settlement. The settlers were, for the most part, well educated, and devoted themselves to transplanting to their new home the culture of their native New England.

Books were scarce and were accorded a welcome which is hard to imagine now. During the early part of that winter a copy of "David Copperfield" arrived in the mail. The most exciting news in the village that day was "Dickens' new novel has come." The owner of the book was generous and the book was liberally loaned. By spring virtually all had read it, and the volume was worn to tatters.

Mr. and Mrs. J. W. North had brought to their home on Nicollet Island a piano, the first in the village. Every week the elect of the colony found their way to the Island across the bridge of accumulated logs, for an evening of music, reading and discussion. About this time William R. Marshall secured the passage of a bill by the legislature authorizing incorporation of a library association. Some two hundred volumes were secured, and the first public library in the State was opened.

The St. Anthony Library Association also sponsored a series of Lyceum lectures. Among the speakers were the Reverend E. D. Neill, the Reverend Ezekiel Gear, William R. Marshall and Lieutenant R. W. Johnson from Fort Snelling. One of the lecturers, a Reverend Mr. Brown, presented in his talk on "Reading and Books" a black-list of fiction to be shunned by decent-thinking people. On this list he unhappily included "Martin Chuzzlewit." The settlers were too well educated to put up with such nonsense, and Brown was taunted until he finally admitted that he had never read the Dickens book but had placed it under ban because the title was displeasing to him.

These New Englanders were church going folks and felt the lack of churches keenly. The Roman Catholics had commenced their church in 1849, but the majority of the settlers were Protestants. The first services were held in the schoolhouse, which was occupied by all denominations in turn. These were strangely mixed congregations, their apparel ranging from high silk hats to coonskin caps and from fine velvets to homespun. The differences in dress did not, however, carry corresponding social distinctions, for the strange land, the mutual hardships and difficulties had brought people close to each other. Reverend E. D. Neill, preaching every other Sunday afternoon, found that his St. Anthony congregations were larger and more attentive than those in St. Paul.

The congregations soon outgrew the schoolhouse, and preparations were made for the organization and erection of a number of churches, to be built with funds from the East. The first Methodist Episcopal Church was organized during the winter of 1849-1850 with Enos Stephens as pastor, although the church building was not started until some time later. The Baptists organized and planned to build the next year, and other sects were encouraged to proceed with their own plans.

While other congregations were striving to build their churches, the Universalists, whose meetings were held in a dismal little hall, were also trying to raise money for this purpose. To this end they held the first church festival in the state, in the autumn of 1855, on Hennepin Island. One feature of this festival was a number of "fine tableaux," and it was some time before the scandal caused by this presentation died down. For a period it was "thought . . . likely some souls would be lost," but times change, and eventually other churches also were holding festivals with tableaux.

St. Paul was becoming a prosperous merchant city, and from its position of unquestioned leadership it looked down on the struggles of little St. Anthony with tolerant but slightly amused eyes. In the spring of 1850, the *Minnesota Pioneer*, leading St. Paul paper of the day, observed that "on Sunday, April 3, a fire broke out in St. Anthony, in the dry grass, and burnt over several squares where the buildings will be."

It was not, to be sure, an impressive place; its growth had been too rapid for an orderly plan, so that it was already an overgrown, sprawling village. Huddled near the river were the newer structures of bright unpainted lumber. Inland were the older dwellings, most of them of logs which had already begun to blacken. There were no imposing buildings. The first problem had been shelter—anything to put a roof over the head. Only after these crude beginnings could the citizens set about building their permanent city.

By 1850 transportation had become the all-important problem of the village. The local merchants, looking with jealous eyes on the flow of trade to St. Paul, began to make plans to divert a part of it to their own doors. Some dreamed of developing commerce to the north. Others coveted the Red River trade which passed tantalizingly close to St. Anthony on its way to St. Paul. Every one was conscious of the need for regular transportation between St. Anthony and St. Paul; settlers had abandoned the village for lack of it, and incoming immigrants had been turned aside. The more ambitious hoped to establish St. Anthony as the head of transportation on the Mississippi—if only they could prevail upon the steamboat captains to disregard the hazards of the river above St. Paul.

The first step was the establishment of a regular stagecoach line between St. Anthony and St. Paul. Early in the summer of 1850, Amherst Willoughby and Simon Powers, who had a small livery business in St. Paul, put a double seated, half-spring wagon, drawn by two horses, into operation as a coach. The enterprise prospered at first, but winter brought it to a halt for lack of a suitable vehicle. In 1851 they put several lumbering, red-painted Concord coaches into operation, each with three seats inside providing space for nine passengers. Baggage and freight were piled on top, behind the driver.

The state of business was such as to attract competition. During 1851 Lyman L. Benson and a Mr. Pattison, two young men recently arrived in St. Paul from Kalamazoo, Michigan, started operation of a better equipped line of large yellow Concord coaches, each drawn by four horses. Both lines ran between the two points twice a day. At first both levied a fare of 50 cents a passenger each way, but then the rivals, popularly known as the "red line" and the "yellow line," began to compete by cutting rates. The differences were settled, however, since there was room and business enough for both.

These coaches ran along an old Indian trail, known as the old Territorial Road. About three miles from St. Anthony on this trail stood a "roadhouse" or tavern belonging to Stephen Desnoyer, where a cool, deep well provided water for the horses, and a bar "quenched the not less thirsty pioneer." This became a popular place for Sunday driving with horses rented from Colonel Allen's livery stable, as well as a stagecoach stop. Also along this road was the Cheever House, where a hydraulic ram had been installed to furnish water for the horses.

Cheever House was on the site which William A. Cheever had platted in 1848 as St. Anthony City, the present grounds of the University of Minnesota. Near his hotel he built a ninety-foot observation tower, where one could "Pay a Dime and Climb" to see the view. The establishment was fairly well patronized and the tower brought in a goodly number of dimes, but the apparent advantages of St. Anthony at the Falls were too great; people went on to that point instead of settling at "Cheevertown."

During 1850 successful attempts were made toward establishing St. Anthony as the head of navigation. On May 4th, Captain Marsh of the steamer *Lamartine* forced his boat to the foot of beautiful Bridal Veil Falls, which then descended sixty feet into the river, some distance below St. Anthony. The *Lamartine* refused to go beyond this strong current, but three days later Captain Rogers succeeded in forcing the *Anthony Wayne* as far as the old rafting place, just below the site of the old Tenth Avenue bridge. The arrival was a great event, the band played, Governor Ramsey and other notables spoke on its significance, and Captain Rogers was presented with a purse of two hundred dollars.

St. Anthony's contention that it was head of navigation was established, but "the only difficulty was that it would not stay established." One pioneer observed that "Nature discountenanced, disfavored, and rendered futile all such artificial efforts." The *Lady Franklin* came near Spirit Island (above Cheever's Landing) later in 1850 and was turned back by the current. No regular steamship service was established until July, 1853, when the *Hindoo* began making trips up as far as Cheever's Landing. River traffic at St. Anthony reached its climax in 1857; fifty-two steamers unloaded there during that year.

There was still the shallow river above the Falls to be conquered, and in this genuine success was achieved. Captain John Rollins, who had a great deal of experience with tough navigation problems, believed that it was possible to build steamboats capable of making the up-river haul. Iron work and machinery were ordered from Maine, shipped by sea to New Orleans and then up the Mississippi. Hull and woodwork were constructed in St. Anthony during the spring of 1850, and on May 25th the steamer *Governor Ramsey* was launched, made a successful trip to Banfield Island, about eight miles, and returned. Next day the boat began making a regular run to Sauk Rapids. During the next decade ten steamships were built at St. Anthony, among them the *Henry M. Rice*, the *Northern Star*, the *Falls City* and the *Enterprise*, and regular service was established to St. Cloud and other northern river points. These boats were built to draw little water; one captain boasted that his craft "would run on a heavy fall of dew."

After 1850, with the transportation problem partially solved, St. Anthony merchants began to succeed in their efforts to secure a share of the region's trade. By 1853 a business directory listed twenty-nine commercial establishments in St. Anthony, and by 1855 the growing village claimed control of the trade in Hennepin County and in sections of Ramsey and Benton Counties as well.

Out of this rapid, confusing growth the institutions and elements of a city began to take shape and form. The St. Charles Hotel was completed in 1850. A two-story building, very large for the period, with accommodations for seventy-five guests, the hotel also provided a ballroom for dancing, and soon became the social center of the village.

Along with other familiar institutions the St. Anthony folk wanted proper and fitting observance of holidays. Especially dear to their New England tradition was Thanksgiving, and in 1850 they waited for Governor Ramsey to proclaim the day. The season passed and no proclamation was forthcoming. Unanimously they decided that Ramsey must be of "Scotch or Dutch pedigree" to have overlooked such an important occasion. A delegation finally visited his office and applied such pressure that he was unable to resist, and he issued a short proclamation. Thanksgiving was observed by a grateful people on the 26th of December.

In the spring of 1851, E. Tyler, a merchant tailor, decided that St. Anthony needed a newspaper. He was strongly advised against the venture, but managed to enlist the reluctant aid of Judge Isaac Atwater as editor, and to secure a press from Chicago, which was set up in a log building. On May 31, 1851, the first issue of the *St. Anthony Express* appeared. This was the only regular chronicle of life in the young city for many years. Money was scarce and many subscribers could pay in produce only, while commercial establishments were slow converts to advertising. Consequently the young men producing the newspaper lived in the printing office and cooked their own meals, which, according to rumor, consisted of mush, milk and molasses.

From its founding, the *St. Anthony Express* was filled with the great expectations common to every pioneer settlement. In the summer of 1851 the paper observed that it required "no very sagacious observer . . . to predict the future of the place. The position which St. Anthony occupies must inevitably make her the great manufacturing and commercial town of the Northwest." These predictions, unlike those of many ebullient frontier newspapers, were to be fulfilled beyond their authors' dreams.

The pioneer newspaper not only expressed the settlers' hopes; it also reflected their moral views. In the *St. Anthony Express* for February 7, 1852, the community spoke its mind in the following terms: "There is not a gambling institution, or a drinking saloon, or a whiskey grocery, or a grog shop in town. We have no room for those who frequent such places." Evidently, with the influx of new settlers, this crusading zeal was lost, for in 1855 the first city council, disregarding the pleas of temperance advocates, licensed the sale of liquor in the community.

The name of St. Anthony, by 1851, had not only spread to the East, but had crossed the sea. It was not the achievements in which its own people took pride, however, that brought this fame—it was the possibilities of the hunt. The region surrounding abounded with game of every kind—gray wolves, wildcats, raccoons, foxes, deer, prairie hens, partridges, and pigeons—yet the country was settled enough so that hunting might be done in comfort and safety. The lack of game laws made the area a sportsman's paradise, and in 1851 there was an invasion of gentleman hunters from many parts of the world. St. Anthony people did not look upon these visitors with pride. As one of them scornfully said, "Lords, Sirs and Honorables were thick as blackberries." The rapid settlement of the community soon reduced the wild life and discouraged the huntsmen.

Immigration steadily increased. Each spring brought a new influx into the territory. In 1852 and 1853 a great many came to St. Anthony; professional and business men moved in to supply the increasing needs of the community. Special mention, also, was made of the fact that "much needed day laborers came."

Despite the swift, frenzied building, there were no vacancies, and the hotel was usually filled. Families, even prosperous ones, were forced to occupy makeshift shelters, for the mill could not turn out lumber fast enough for the buyers who were waiting. Business establishments in St. Anthony and St. Paul tried vainly to keep up with the demands of a rapidly growing population.

Lumbering developed at a tremendous pace; it was the major interest of the community. A prediction that any other industry would rival or surpass it would have been ridiculed. By the summer of 1851, sixteen saws were turning out 50,000 feet of lumber a day. The manufacture of lath and shingles alone provided employment for 100 men. Each year the capacity of the mills increased and more logs came down the river to the Falls.

Ever since the establishment of the old Government grist mill across the river, the milling of grain had been regarded as more of a convenience than an industry worthy of development. In 1851 R. C. Rogers built, at the end of the row of lumber mills, a rude grist mill which was improved with "two run of stone" the next year. In the main, this mill was for use of the farmers in the vicinity. In 1854 a larger mill was opened, but there was not enough wheat to keep it running until some was brought from Iowa, by river-boat and wagon. Flour, in common with most agricultural products, still had to be imported. Although farmers in swiftly increasing numbers were discovering the richness of Minnesota soil, it was necessary as late as 1853 to import such necessities as butter, lard and pork, as well as hay for livestock. And it was several years later before any degree of self-sufficiency was reached.

In the spring of 1854, the Winnebago Indians passed through St. Anthony on their way from Watab to the Blue Earth Reservation. In return for pennies, cold lunches and gifts they performed their tribal dances and sang their strange songs. One Sunday morning during their stay a prankster told them that the people who lived in a certain big house would enjoy their dancing and would reward them liberally. This "big house" was the Methodist Episcopal Church, in which the Reverend Creighton was conducting the regular morning service. The Indians, somewhat skeptical, crept up and peered in the windows. Although the people of St. Anthony had never suffered an Indian attack, there had been plenty of frontier tales to make them nervous. When in the midst of the sermon the worshippers glanced up and saw the Indians looking in, the service came to an abrupt end, for the congregation fled from the church, leaving the minister puzzled and dismayed. The joke was discovered, but worship was not resumed that morning.

In its first year of operation, 1847, the ferry netted a return of $300. This income increased with the years, until the growing settlement on the west side of the river began to make too great demands upon the meager equipment of the ferry line. In 1854 the Minneapolis Bridge Company, of which Franklin Steele was the leading spirit, was incorporated. Its purpose was to build a bridge across the Mississippi, the first bridge to span that mighty stream.

This structure, designed as a single arch supported by cables, was built under the supervision of T. J. Griffith, an engineer from Fort Snelling. By December 14, 1854, E. H. Conner, a foreman, and five or six workmen crossed on the loose planking. After that, foot passengers were allowed to cross at ten cents each. In March, in a blasting storm, the bridge swayed so violently that the planking cracked up under the strain. To prevent a repetition of this disaster, supporting guy wires were placed on each side, attached to piers, to hold the structure steady. This delayed the completion of the bridge until July 4, 1855. Upon this date the first team crossed, followed by a procession and a celebration.

The opening of this bridge marked a turning point which few men of that time recognized. That same year St. Anthony was incorporated as a city, and because of its manufacturing importance, it seemed that it might become the dominant city of the river. St. Paul had already altered its tone from condescending humor to bitterness, for St. Anthony had grown to be a menacing, aggressive rival. But industry and trade crossed this bridge also, and the real rival of St. Paul became the newer city on the western shore. Here Minneapolis, of which St. Anthony would be but a part, was to rise.

From These Wildernesses
The Growth of Minneapolis

The land on the west side of the river, near the Fort, had been settled upon at different times by missionaries, traders and squatters. The missionaries went on to other duties, the traders moved to more opportune fields, and the refugees from the Selkirk colonies were removed by military force after they had built their little homes and put the land under cultivation.

Despite the fact that the area was part of the military reservation and subject to the jurisdiction of the authorities of Fort Snelling, men dreamed always of taking land there. It was the most attractive spot in the region, and obviously it was certain to become an important townsite. But it was as hard to get as it was attractive.

After earlier attempts to secure the land by more honorable means had met with failure, political influence finally opened the way. On February 15, 1849, Robert Smith, Congressman from Illinois, asked the authorities in Washington for permission to lease the old Government grist mill and house for a period of five years. "I shall move into the Territory of Minnesota after the adjournment of Congress," he wrote, "and I wish to secure this house for my family to live in, and to fix up the old grist mill to grind corn . . . " His request was approved, with the provision that the commandant of Fort Snelling also give his consent. Major Woods, then in command at the Fort, grudgingly gave his approval but expressed his suspicion as to Mr. Smith's real purpose. "I doubt much if his aim in wishing to settle there is not in expectation that the reserve will be taken off." Smith took possession in May but did not bring his family to the territory and did not live there himself. After inspecting the land he wrote again to the Secretary of War, requesting additional land for raising other provisions. This request, too, was granted.

Major Woods' suspicions were amply justified, for although Smith visited the place he never operated it himself, and year after year he returned to Congress from his district in Illinois. He put one Reuben Bean in charge of the property. Bean, with his family, lived in the dwelling formerly occupied by the miller from the Fort. It was years before Smith undertook any development of the site, yet his occupation of the land was important, for it was the opening wedge for further settlement.

Colonel John H. Stevens, with a party of ten, arrived in St. Anthony on Friday, April 27, 1849, in search of a site for an agricultural colony. It was typical of the times that among his supplies Stevens brought 38 gallons of whiskey. According to his contemporaries the Colonel was not a drinking man, but he had "brought the whiskey with him to have a remedy on hand in case he was bitten by a snake, and to have it in his power to extend the usual western hospitality."

Stevens and his companions ranged northward along the eastern shore of the river. They were terribly disappointed in the soil, which was sandy, not like the rich black earth of their native Illinois. Though they were shown fine crops raised from this sandy soil, it still would not do for them.

On the other side of the river, however, they found the type of soil they most desired, and this proved the crowning disappointment of the expedition, for it was doubly forbidden land; the Indians and the military each had a claim upon it. The party disbanded then, and each man went his own way. Stevens decided to go to St. Paul and then to Fort Snelling. He had traveled through the land on the west side of the river near the Fort and was impressed by its beauty and its promise. This was the land he wanted—and could not have.

At the Fort, Stevens became postmaster, an important position in the Territory. But of even more consequence was the fact that he met Franklin Steele. If any man could help him obtain land west of the river, it was Steele, for Steele, more than anyone else, was the power at the Fort and at St. Anthony. Steele found he could rely upon Stevens, for almost from their first meeting the Colonel became an immoderate admirer of the ambitious and enterprising sutler.

On a June morning in 1849, Steele asked Stevens to go with him to the Falls. On this journey, Steele confided that the military reservation was to be reduced in size and that it might be possible to secure from the Secretary of War permission to take up a claim to which title could be confirmed after the reservation was reduced. A congressman from Illinois had secured land; Stevens, with Steele's aid, could do the same. A claim was staked out, to the north of Smith's and equally valuable from the standpoint of potential water power control. Steele's influence evidently carried weight, for Secretary of War Marcy readily consented to the occupancy.

Just above the rapids, on the bank of the river, Stevens built the first permanent private residence on the western side of the river, approximately on the location of the present railway express terminal. It was one and a half stories high, with white painted clapboard siding and a broad veranda overlooking the river—a New England farmhouse transplanted in lonely isolation. It was surrounded by trees, and soon lilacs were planted. In this dwelling almost every activity of the future settlement first was sheltered. It served in turn as hotel, meeting place, church, land office, bank and theatre.

Earlier in that year of 1849, Philander Prescott, trader, farmer and interpreter, had attempted to stake a claim on the forbidden ground, on what is now the east side of Minnehaha Avenue. He, however, was not allowed to remain. Later Franklin Steele took possession of this claim.

In the winter of the same year, Charles Mousseaux, with permission of the Fort authorities, settled on a piece of land on the eastern shore of Lake Calhoun. He erected a shanty where the Pond brothers' mission had once stood, and he was not disturbed in his claim. He was a long distance from the power site, so far away indeed that not even the wildest dreamer would have guessed that the spot was so soon to be embraced within the limits of a great city.

Stevens' claim aroused a good deal of speculation. St. Anthony people predicted that a town would be started soon on the western shore. James M. Goodhue, indefatigable booster of St. Paul, tried to quench these ambitions of his neighbors under a flood of editorial derision in his *Minnesota Pioneer*. On February 27, 1850, he laughed at the exaggerated hopes of the people of the east shore settlement, suggesting that the non-existent city across the river "be called 'All Saints,' so as to head off the whole calendar of Saints." But these earnest men sometimes acted seriously upon suggestions meant as jibes, and All Saints was accepted for a time as the name of the settlement.

In the spring of 1850 Stevens brought a drove of ten good cows from Muscatine, Iowa, at a cost, including transportation, of eleven dollars each. In the summer he took up the plow and turned forty acres of the fine prairie sod, and the following year these acres bore a prime crop of wheat, corn, oats, buckwheat, potatoes and vegetables. When Stevens came, there were only some three hundred farms in the entire Territory of Minnesota, and there was little interest in agriculture on the northwest frontier. Stevens' farm, however, impressed many of the incoming immigrants, and attracted them to the land to the west of the river. They regarded the future site of Minneapolis as a fine farming region, and the earliest settlement on the west bank was laid out with that in view. The utmost the founders hoped for was that their community might be recognized in time as a suburb of the industrial city of St. Anthony. However, it was not long before more imaginative men visioned an imposing city, for they saw its industrial possibilities, as well as its fertile soil.

Stevens moved into his house August 6, 1850. Soon afterwards he brought his family there, and on a cold bleak day in April of the next year, his daughter Mary was born. That year other permanent settlers came and the anxious, tragic struggle for land began.

Not every man could reach the ear of the Secretary of War to secure permission to take up land on the Reserve. In the autumn of 1850 Dr. Hezekiah Fletcher of Maine was allowed to stake out a claim. He chose one "far back," on what is now Portland Avenue between 14th and 15th streets. John Jackins was the next settler. The land he chose, and on which he built a small house, lay just back of Stevens' claim. A group of men, among them Allan Harmon and Dr. A. E. Ames, arrived in 1851 with permits to take up claims.

Stevens' example gave courage to others. Forbidden ground did not seem so forbidding after one man had taken possession without penalty. It was better land, and pioneers were not timid men. During the winter of 1851-52 rumors spread even to eastern states that the reduction of the Reserve was impending, and settlers came prepared to file claims on the west side of the river.

In the spring claims were staked, rude and clumsy shanties were built, and the more ambitious claimants broke small patches of land. These were intended as indications of proposed possession, but later they became tests of the feasibility of settlement, for it was evident that unless an agreement with the military authorities could be reached, it was a hopeless fight. All who maintained claims before the land was released did so under official permits or with the connivance of the post authorities. Friends of Steele seemed to have little to worry about, aside from the usual hardships of pioneer existence.

A war for possession followed, one in which would-be settlers faced unequal odds. Men crossed the frozen ice in winter to "the Canaan of their hopes" and blazed trees to mark off claims they hoped to win for themselves. Most of them were without the influence to secure permits, but hoped that sheer daring might serve. Officers at the Fort were both tyrannical and corrupt. Settlers were told that they must turn over a half interest in the claim at time of entry. Those who refused met with misfortune. At two different times, shanties were torn down and improvements destroyed by soldiers. Some claimants gave up in face of the heavy odds against them, but others stubbornly returned and built again.

Thus, across the river from St. Anthony, Minnesota witnessed its own version of the land rush, smaller in scale than others in western frontier history, but equally fierce and bitter. Such a land rush was apt to occur wherever legal barriers held off for a time the natural flow of settlement and immigration. Behind such barriers the prospective settlers gathered like water behind a dam, and the moment the barrier was swept away, like angry waters they surged out over the land. Friendship and fellow feeling counted for nothing; a loophole in a neighbor's claim made him a legitimate victim. It was not safe to leave a claim cabin empty even for a few minutes; the claimant might return to find the shack occupied by a "jumper" who could be removed only with violence or money. Sometimes it was necessary to guard a cabin with rifles, night and day.

To protect themselves from "jumping," the actual settlers organized an "Equal Right and Impartial Protection Claim Association," and a committee was set up to act on all disputes about claims. Measures so severe that no jumper "could be sure of his life" were threatened by the claim association. When threats proved insufficient, a cat-o'-nine-tails was laid across the naked back of one trespasser, the only instance of actual violence, but one which impressed "jumpers." Of course, there was none too much "right" on either side, since legally, with few exceptions, all were trespassers. Therefore compromise was often necessary.

Because of their high hopes for its future, the name of the new city was of great importance. All Saints had been accepted in some quarters; others felt that it did not lend proper dignity nor distinction. Albion was suggested. Practical businessmen wanted the name Lowell, since they believed the new settlement might become the textile center of the west. A gallant proposed that it be called Adasville in compliment to a local belle, Ada Hoag. John Stevens proposed honoring the earlier pioneers by naming the village Hennepin and the county Snelling. Winona was also considered.

At first the name Albion found official favor, and when Hennepin County was organized in 1852, the County Commissioners selected that name for the settlement, and the County Clerk entered it in the records. This action met with general disapproval, and was overruled by popular feeling. Many letters went out from the community datelined All Saints. The controversy was heated, each group staunchly championing its choice, until on November 5, 1852, in an article in the *St. Anthony Express*, Charles Hoag, a teacher "not unfamiliar with letters," proposed the name "Minnehapolis." "This name, with its nice adjustment of the Indian *minne* with the Greek *polis*" found immediate favor with all factions. The "h" was dropped to make the word more musical, and the new city became Minneapolis.

The first Minneapolis school was opened late in 1851, in an old lumbermen's shanty on the Anson Northup claim, near the present Milwaukee station. Miss Mary A. Scofield was the teacher. There were very few pupils, but by December 3, 1852, when Miss Mary E. Miller took over the school, the number had grown. But however great the need, no schoolhouse could be built, since legal title to the land could not be secured. Miss Hartwell started a second school in July, 1852, in a frame building on the corner of Hennepin Avenue and Fourth Street. Though this building was larger, it did not prove much better for the purpose than the smaller one near the river, for it had been boarded with green lumber and the siding had curled. By fall, wind and rain were whipping through the cracks, and the school was forced to move to the parlor of John Jackins' home, where the term was completed.

Ard Godfrey, one of the early St. Anthony settlers, was also attracted by land on the west side of the river. In 1853 he preempted 160 acres lying between Minnehaha Creek and the Mississippi, and later erected a small sawmill at the mouth of the creek.

During the latter part of 1853, Thomas Chambers opened the Pioneer Store on what is now Bridge Square, so that the settlers no longer had to cross by ferry and trade in St. Anthony.

By 1854 settlement had proceeded far enough to make a survey of the entire townsite necessary, and William R. Marshall was secured to do the job. The plat was never recorded, however, due to the fact that there were no clear titles to the property.

Until this year, residents on the west side of the river received and sent mail through the post office at St. Anthony. Now Dr. Fletcher was appointed Minneapolis postmaster, but there was no arrangement for extending delivery of mail to the new settlement. Dr. A. E. Ames, whose duties frequently took him to St. Anthony, made a practice of bringing the mail back with him, in his pockets or in his hat. It was a year and a half before the government extended its route to Minneapolis. The "post office" was in Dr. Fletcher's office on the corner of First and Helen Streets.

Many citizens of the new settlement had confidence in the future of Minnesota as an agricultural state. They had claimed their property as farm land, and planned to use it for that purpose. Early in the 1850's they formed the Hennepin County Agricultural Society, which opened the first agricultural fair in the state on October 20, 1854. It was held on the present site of Bridge Square, which was the important center of Minneapolis life. The fair was addressed by many distinguished men, and visitors and settlers alike were impressed by the showing made. The *St. Anthony Express* commented that it "would have done credit to one of the oldest and richest agricultural counties in New York."

The government, or at least the military authorities, had placed every possible obstacle in the way of settlement, but as the time for the reduction of the Reserve and the legal opening of the land grew near, it appeared that there was an even more formidable opposition on the outside. In 1854 it was announced that the plats were to be forwarded from Washington and lots sold at auction to the highest bidder. This was the usual procedure, but in this case it was likely to deprive the original claimants of their land. The region was now so well settled that it was easy to foresee the future importance of this townsite. Land speculators from the east, attracted by this new promise of rich and easy "pickings," were already swarming into St. Paul, so that in an open sale the claimants could hardly hope to compete successfully with the speculators.

It was not in the nature of these men to sit idly by and see themselves deprived of their homes and hopes. Moreover they did not intend to pay more than the standard government price of $1.25 an acre for preemption claims. They had dealt with the "jumpers"; they felt they could deal with speculators. In this new crisis they turned again to the Claim Association. Thomas W. Pierce was selected as bidder for the organization, and all of the members were instructed to gather at the sale so that they might intimidate, by force if necessary, any speculators bold enough to bid. Public opinion was strongly with the settlers, and it was hinted that Governor Gorman would call out the militia to handle the situation.

The plats did not arrive on schedule, however, and the sale had to be postponed. This gave the Association a little time, and a committee was sent to Washington to protest the unjust procedure of the public sale. The men departed for Washington on October 9, 1854. At first they met only with rebuffs, but finally their persistence won a stay of proceedings from the Secretary of the Interior. Dr. Ames, a member of the committee, remained in Washington and was at last successful in securing from Congress a reduction of the Reserve and a provision allowing the actual settlers to buy the land at $1.25 per acre. April and May of 1855 saw a happy conclusion of the struggle for the land; the settlers proved their claims and development began in earnest. At the completion of preemptions in 1855, there was not a quarter section in the entire county which was not occupied by actual settlers.

Another important matter stirred the settlers to organized action in 1854. A temperance league was formed, determined that no "drunkard maker" should be allowed in the village, and a $9,000 fund raised for the purpose of applying "moral and legal suasion" to this end.

Business and industrial development had been seriously retarded, of course, by the uncertainty of permanent ownership of the land. When this obstacle was removed a building boom immediately ensued. Lots were selling at a premium, and stores, churches, homes, and shops were built at feverish speed. Cottages began to replace the log cabins. By autumn more than 100 buildings had been erected.

In both St. Anthony and Minneapolis the real estate business promised such golden rewards that men of all professions abandoned their regular callings for it. These were boom days in Minneapolis, and along with sound industrial and mercantile development there was speculation, with high prices and fabulous interest rates.

On March 4, 1856, St. Anthony was detached from Ramsey County and made a part of Hennepin County, and during the same year an act of the legislature provided for the incorporation of the town of Minneapolis. The first platted map of Minneapolis was produced in 1857 by Orlando Talcott. As if to prove their existence, a number of the most impressive structures reared during the year were sketched in meticulous detail on the margin of the map. The most impressive and expensive of these buildings was the Nicollet House, which had been constructed at the corner of Hennepin and Washington Avenues at a cost of $50,000. The year had increased the number of buildings to 444. Minneapolis and St. Anthony now had approximately the same population, somewhat over 4,000, yet the $512,000 spent for new buildings in Minneapolis that year was almost double the total expended for the same purpose in St. Anthony.

That year a brick schoolhouse was finished—"the best school building north of St. Louis." Unfortunately it was not allowed to serve the community long. From the beginning, the citizens were determined to provide decent school facilities for their children, and a mass meeting had been called for that purpose in 1854. Nothing definite was accomplished at that time, but the next year they petitioned the legislature to authorize a loan for the erection of a school. The legislature approved the request in March, 1856, and in May the townsfolk voted to erect a two-story brick schoolhouse, and bought the land for it.

The fine new building was destroyed by fire in the early 1860's. Two Scottish school boys had been severely punished by a schoolmaster who was an extreme disciplinarian. Shortly afterward the fire occurred. At the same time the boys' parents, who had angrily resented the severity of their sons' punishment, disappeared overnight with all their family. It was believed, of course, that this family had started the fire. In any case, the community had to start all over again with plans for a new school.

That same eventful year brought to the west river community its first newspaper, when W. A. Hotchkiss purchased the *Northwestern Democrat*, published in St. Anthony since 1853, and moved it to Minneapolis. But although the community was large enough to support a newspaper, this one survived only a short time.

It was at the dizzy height of the land craze that the financial panic of 1857 struck the nation, and dealt severely with the cities at the Falls. Real estate lost about one third of its valuation. Wages dived from $1.50 per day to 90 cents. Imports into the territory dropped 50 per cent in a year. Real estate speculators were ruined by tumbling prices, and hundreds of smaller fortunes were wiped out within a few months. Towns which had been bustling with activity and alive with ambitious dreams a short time before relapsed into utter stagnation.

The few lumber workers who were employed during the winter of 1857 did not receive pay which had been promised them. Early the following summer they elected a committee of twelve to demand these wages, and in desperation they threatened to cut the boom, release the accumulated logs and sell them down river, if they were not paid. But even this dire threat was ineffectual, for the entire community had been stricken by the same blight.

There was not enough money in circulation to carry on ordinary business, and "wildcat paper" was printed for use as currency. Hennepin County issued $6,000 worth of script, and the city of St. Anthony $5,000. This was expected to "relieve many a poor man." At first the merchants were reluctant to accept this substitute money, and did so only after they found that they must either be paid in script or "trust their goods out, or keep them in their stores, suffering a depreciation." Even lumber sometimes served as a medium of circulation.

Before the panic, there had been an announcement that a competitor city might enter the race with St. Anthony, Minneapolis and St. Paul. Franklin Steele had purchased the Fort Snelling site, at the convergence of the Minnesota and Mississippi rivers, and since in those days river transportation was so decisive a factor, it looked as if this settlement, which Steele planned to call Minnesota City, might become a dangerous rival. But Steele's plan which had made the three cities a "little nervous" was completely shattered by the financial panic.

The next year the following item appeared in the *Daily Minnesotian:* "MONEY GETTING PLENTIER . . . A gentleman yesterday informed us that three persons voluntarily came to him and paid some accounts in good currency. What's broke loose?" The headline was hardly warranted by business conditions, which were showing only a gradual improvement.

The panic, though it brought disaster to so many people, did not have an entirely adverse effect on the cities themselves. It actually increased their control of Northwest trade, and served to deflate unhealthy speculation. The "late revulsion" was also of indirect benefit in that it brought a new influx of settlers. Throughout the East, people who had been ruined by the disaster were turning westward, and there were few adventurers or fortune hunters among them. They were common folk, homeseekers and homebuilders. It was said of such immigration that it "will mark an epoch in our history, and will be of more advantage to us than so many speculators and schemers who bring no wealth into the country . . . and can never create any."

The year 1857 marked the opening of the first place in which theatrical performances were held. Ivory T. Woodman opened Woodman's Hall, on Washington and Second Avenue S., with a dazzling presentation of *Uncle Tom's Cabin* by the Sallie St. Clair Troupe. Another milestone had been marked the year before with the visit to Minneapolis of the child songstress Adelina Patti, who came up the river on a concert tour with Ole Bull, the famous violinist.

Town government was organized in Minneapolis in 1858, and H. T. Welles was elected president of the city council. This first form of government was continued for four years but proved to be impractical. It was abandoned for the simpler township form, which was used until the incorporation of the city.

Development continued steadily, though it was far too slow for those impatient ones who had been nourished on the wild speculation of the decade before. Eastern capital now came in, and business enterprises began to be placed on a more solid basis. An instance of the influx of eastern money was the establishment of the first bank in St. Anthony, December, 1858, by Miles A. Bradley of New York.

From the earliest days, vacationists had been attracted by the natural beauties of Minnesota. First Fort Snelling, and now the towns at the Falls, attracted visitors from every section of the United States. By 1856 the existing boarding houses and hotels were crowded beyond capacity, and in 1857 Captain James M. Winslow began construction of an elaborate hotel in St. Anthony, high on the bank above the river. A dignified building of gray stone, no effort was spared to make it a place of luxury and ease. To complete its elegance a gold-plated archangel weathervane was mounted on a flagpole in front of the building. The archangel had been made in Lyons, France, for the French exhibit at an American exposition, after which it mysteriously disappeared. Winslow discovered it in the possession of a trader in Wisconsin.

Before the hotel was completed it was considered too ambitious and adventurous a scheme. One newspaper commented that it was in "typical Winslow style—with a cupola and mortgage on top." Friendlier prophets, however, predicted that "it would be surpassed by no house in the United States." The critics were confounded by the hotel's brilliant success. At one event, the celebration of the opening of the railroad to LaCrosse, 500 guests were entertained in the sumptuous banquet rooms.

A pageant of Southern tourists with their Negro slaves moved up the river to the cities at the Falls. In addition to the enjoyment of the river voyage, they came to view Minnehaha Falls, Lake Minnetonka, the Minneapolis chain of lakes and the rugged bluffs of the Upper Mississippi. On the eastern bank of the river, not far from the Winslow House, "the old Chalybeate Springs" drew many to drink of their supposedly beneficial mineral waters. In these "palmy days," Southern belles in crinoline and gentlemen in attire more elegant than the villagers had ever seen crowded the log platform and the wooden steps leading to the springs.

[51]

Once the hotel was a proven success, Winslow, who had irons in many fires, sold it to C. W. McLean for the record sum of $160,000.

For Winslow it had been a surprisingly profitable venture, but McLean was not so lucky. The course of history conspired against him. Intellectual conviction became passion as Northerners felt their interests and freedom endangered by the spread of slavery. As early as June 1854, a call had been circulated for an anti-slavery convention in St. Anthony; the announcement set forth the issues with wrathy clarity. "A systematic and high handed attempt is being made to 'crush out' the spirit of liberty from the land, and to diffuse, nationalize and perpetuate slavery. The North is sinking into a degraded vassalage, through the defection of its own public men." The convention was held in the Congregational Church at St. Anthony on July 4th. The "radical views" of civic and religious leaders such as John North, the Reverend C. G. Ames and the Reverend Charles Secombe were given expression. The next year Ames founded the *St. Anthony Republican*, which was strongly abolitionist in tone, and reflected the increasing anti-slavery sentiment.

The display of Negro slaves by Southerners increased the heat of the controversy. Those whose business prosperity depended upon the tourist trade became ardent Southern partisans. Abolitionists pointedly warned such as these to moderate their views, suggesting that they "put gold on one scale and liberty on the other" and see which weighed the more.

At length the abolitionists determined upon a demonstration which would inform Negroes of their rights in Minnesota. Eliza Winston, a Negro nursemaid, who had traveled North with Colonel Christmas and his family, was informed that she could not be forced to return to the South in servitude. The case was argued before the court in August 1860 and the woman was freed.

That evening, Southern partisans gathered in a menacing throng about the house of W. D. Babbitt, where Miss Winston had been given shelter, loudly demanding that she be returned to her master. The house was barricaded against them, and in the half light of early morning she was taken to a safer refuge by Frank Stone, superintendent of schools. Eventually she fled to Canada. The Southern tourist trade slackened as a result of this affair and the anti-slavery opinion which it represented, and the Winslow House began to lose its fashionable trade.

Business conditions as a whole had not recovered completely from the disaster of 1857. As Mrs. Ard Godfrey wrote to her sister in Maine in 1861, "times have been hard in Minnesota for the past three years: but all feel in hopes the coming year will bring a change . . . money is scarce."

Despite set-backs, Minneapolis and St. Anthony were well settled cities by 1860. On the west side of the river it had not been entirely certain where the business center of the town should be located, but gradually the choice seemed to focus on Bridge Square, since the suspension bridge forced commerce through that channel. Facing the Square stood the Nicollet House, Minneapolis' most imposing inn, while on either side were straggling one-story shops and stores. In the center of it all was a mud puddle, known as the "goose pond." One of the features of the square was the lending library of Thomas Hale Williams, in a book store. Later this was moved into the Center Block, where it was known as the Athenaeum and became the foundation of the present public library.

The rivals of Bridge Square were the few stores along Twentieth Avenue North, and the stores about the Cataract House at Washington and Sixth Avenue South. It was years before Nicollet Avenue was considered a business street, and Hennepin's highest hope was to become a fashionable residential district. The business streets boasted wooden sidewalks; elsewhere there were only packed dirt paths, which in wet weather turned to sticky mud.

On the other side of the river St. Anthony had expanded. With the Winslow House on the high ground above the river bank, and the increasing number of mills, it was the more impressive of the two cities. However, little had been done to develop the University. Only Old Main Hall had been erected, and now it had neither faculty nor students.

As 1861 opened, the accumulated bitterness of years of sectional controversy neared the point of open conflict between the newly-formed Confederacy and the Federal Union. Even before the forces of the Confederacy had fired upon Fort Sumter, a meeting of Minneapolis citizens had offered to enlist "to aid in the protection of the flag of our country." When President Lincoln called for troops to defend the Union, Minneapolis men responded gallantly and enthusiastically. A newspaper in a neighboring city describes one defense meeting as follows: "A great mass meeting of the citizens of Old Hennepin was held in Bridge Square today, to consider our present troubles. A stand was erected near the Liberty Pole, at the top of which, floating in the breeze, was the glorious Stars and Stripes, which was saluted again and again by our enthusiastic young men, who, in the absence of a field piece, burnt their powder in six large anvils . . . " Some carried military enthusiasm to such excess that boys under fifteen years of age were being instructed in the use of the broadsword.

The war brought a new interruption to the progress of the communities at the Falls. Even had there been capital available for further investments the labor supply was so depleted that no work could be undertaken. Women and boys were employed in many places. Trade was paralyzed. Farmers used old tools and equipment, and bought only the barest essentials on their infrequent trips to town.

River traffic came to a standstill. The boats which had operated above St. Anthony Falls were sold to the Government for use as transports on the shallow rivers of the Southwest. The Southern tourist trade had now stopped completely, and the elegant Winslow House was closed and its furnishings sold. Telegraph wires had reached Minneapolis in 1860, so news of the war was not lacking. This news was the major interest of those who remained at home.*

The falling off of river transportation made a railroad imperative for the life of the towns. Action had been pending on this problem since 1853, but through mismanagement or misfortune every promotional plan had failed. The intense desire for railroad facilities had led the legislature to make a number of unwise commitments. Early in 1862 the St. Paul and Pacific Railway was chartered by the State, and took over the properties of the old Minnesota and Pacific venture. That spring there was not a mile of completed railway trackage in the entire State; a few stretches of neglected, weed-covered grading, where the going had been easy, were the only visible evidence of the ambitious project. In early summer, though, ten miles of track connecting St. Anthony and St. Paul were completed. On June 28, 1862, a trial run was made with a woodburning locomotive, called the *William Crooks*, and two coaches. This was the first successful railroad construction in the State, and was placed in regular operation July 2nd. Fare was 45 cents each way, including free transportation to hotels.

This coming of the first railroad seemed to mark 1862 as an auspicious year on the Northwest frontier. Yet it was in that same year that one of Minnesota's great tragedies occurred. With the Civil War in progress and the soldiers engaged far from Minnesota, the Sioux Indians thought they saw the one last opportunity to save their vanishing lands. The Sioux Outbreak, which began in Redwood in August, terrorized white settlements throughout Minnesota and brought hundreds of panic driven refugees into Minneapolis, even from such nearby points as Excelsior. They came in wagons with a few hastily collected belongings, driving their livestock, and the people of Minneapolis organized to feed and shelter them until the danger was over. Whatever military power the Sioux possessed was crushed by their defeat at Wood Lake on September 23, 1862, and the frontier once more returned to peaceful activities.

* Hale, Mary Thayer, *Early Minneapolis*, Page 16. Parsons, *Story of Minneapolis*, (Page 69) implies that there was no telegraph at this time and that news was brought by steamboat. Hale is corroborated by the following: Folwell, W. W., *History of Minnesota*, Vol. 2, pp. 65, 66; *St. Anthony Falls Evening News*, Nov. 17, 1860.

After the close of the Civil War came a period of swift, almost breakneck expansion. All industries, including the railroads, made great strides forward. Developments that had been withheld during the years of the panic and the war now went forward with unbelievable swiftness. Once more immigrants were streaming into the Northwest. Settlement extended to the Dakota Territory, thus opening a new market to the cities. Agricultural production rose, and there were increased demands also for the products of the cities. Railroad expansion strove vainly to keep up with settlement.

During the 1860's St. Paul still maintained her unquestioned trade and commercial leadership. Minneapolis and St. Anthony might resent this fact, but their own rapid industrial progress during this period was due in large part to the very fact that they were situated next door to the premier city of the Northwest.

Other ambitious towns of the State considered themselves rivals of the three cities. Stillwater, Hastings, Red Wing, St. Peter and Winona, each in its day had hopes of emerging as the center of the northwestern empire. But none could offer the inducements available in St. Paul, Minneapolis and St. Anthony, so that one by one they receded into the background, to assume the relatively obscure role of trade tributaries.

Minneapolis and St. Paul now began their long contest to see which should become the railway center of the State. When the first railroad reached Minneapolis proper in September 1865, a local editor proclaimed, over his front page, "A NEW ERA! Minneapolis Opened To The World! MINNEAPOLIS THE MAGNET OF THE WEST! The immortal has triumphed over the perishable, the celestial over the terrestial . . . The Minnesota Central Railway has reached its terminus—Minneapolis! . . . Destiny, always moving among the sources of power, will build here the Lawrence and Lowell of the West, and to us will come the great multitude." This and similar outbursts elicited the sour comment from a St. Paul newspaper that "if it [Minneapolis] is a magnet, it is a poor one, for it don't draw."

Horace Greeley visited Minneapolis at this time and wrote a series of impressions for his paper in New York. "St. Paul has some 13,000 inhabitants, while this place, including St. Anthony's Falls . . . has some 8,000 and there seems to be a jealous rivalry between them which is absurd . . . MINNEAPOLIS HAS ADVANTAGE ENOUGH IN HER ENORMOUS WATER POWER . . . it has no superior but Niagara." This enthusiastic report caught the attention of the nation.

Meanwhile Minneapolis was shouting her own praises to all who would listen. A vague excitement hung over the city—anything might happen. It was a wonderful world, full of surprising and very profitable opportunities. The newspapers reflected this breathless, naive wonder in dispatches like the following: "Do you know, fellow citizens, that business is actually being carried on in this town in the night time by an illuminating fluid called Gas? . . . It is one of the privileges of Minneapolis, that she is not likely to be cursed with such gas companies as dominate over large cities . . . a gas extracted from petroleum may prove of great service to her, because it can be manufactured by the consumer." This was one of the "privileges" of early Minneapolis that was not to last.

No other business rose to such extremes of madness as real estate. It was serious advice, seriously given, when property holders of Minneapolis were told to "strike while the iron is hot. So long as there is a demand for real estate, you must advance your prices and valuations, one thousand per cent if necessary, and perhaps you will get them . . . The goose that lays the golden eggs has been seen on different lots by trustworthy individuals. She is going her rounds . . ."

While St. Anthony had been the scene of the earliest and most spectacular development in lumber milling, Minneapolis soon equaled its activity. Together the mills built or in building by 1857 were estimated to have a combined annual capacity of 60 to 75 million feet of lumber. Thirteen thousand shingles and 20,000 lath were turned out daily, and about 150,000,000 feet of logs were brought down the river that year.

There was ample power, and the timber supply seemed to be inexhaustible. Lumber was turned out in larger quantities than could be used by the Minnesota communities, thriving and multiplying as they were. However, there was a ready market down the river, at St. Louis and points south. The lumber was put up in huge rafts, containing from one million to two million feet, and floated down. These clumsy affairs, sometimes drawn by steam tugs, sometimes borne with the current, were guided by big stern oars that kept them in the channel and prevented them from being broken on shallows, bars and curving banks.

By 1865 the space on the banks of the river in both towns was taken up by flour and lumber mills, and mills were being built away from the river, to be operated by steam power. Five years later 118 million feet of lumber was cut, and production was still on the upgrade.

Every fall the city would ring to the lusty carousals, the songs, stories, and highly skilled "cussing" of the lumberjacks, awaiting departure to the winter camps in the northern woods. In March the scarlet-and-green-shirted clan would throng the city again, a winter's pay in their pockets, eager for the delights of the city which had been denied them through the drear, long winter. Soon they were broke again—out of a job until the ice went out in April, until the saws once more began to hum and smoke reappeared in the mill chimneys.

The coming and going of the lumberjacks marked the seasons for Minneapolis as surely as a flight of geese or a budding tree. They were criticized as wasteful and wild and looked upon with disdain by more respectable citizens. Yet lumbering, which could not have existed without these men, was even then laying the financial base upon which industry in Minneapolis and agriculture in the surrounding area were to be developed.

Agriculture was now well established, and Minnesota had begun exporting agricultural products. Potatoes and wheat were shipped out in constantly larger quantities. The towns at the Falls, of course, shared in this trade. It was said in May 1860, that "upwards of 30,000 bushels of grain and potatoes are, we learn, in store at St. Anthony and Minneapolis awaiting shipments, and as soon as any chance is seen for removal of this quantity, its place will immedately be filled with other thousands from up river and the back country."

By 1861 the quality of its wheat was bringing widespread recognition of Minnesota's place in cereal production. Some milling had been done in St. Anthony, but in the first years it was not looked upon as a potentially important industry. As early as 1856 an editor thought it was "about time that we should stop importing the 'staff of life' from the States below." There was only one substantial mill in Minneapolis, the Minnesota Mill, which had been built by Eastman, Rollins and Upton on the lower end of Hennepin Island in 1854. This enterprise was profitable enough to strengthen the conviction that no more flour should be imported, and in 1858 it actually exported an experimental shipment of 125 barrels, foreshadowing the huge trade which was to follow.

By 1861 more mills were in operation, and Minneapolis and St. Anthony were prepared to ship 3,000 barrels of flour to St. Louis that season. The Civil War made the demand imperative, and brought about an increase in the farming areas, so that the supply of grain became more plentiful and dependable. Seven years later the Minneapolis mills were turning out 3,000 barrels a day and railroads were running entire trainloads of flour and lumber from the city.

The city was also becoming a center for other agricultural products. Two hundred and eighty teams hauling wood, hay and farm produce were reported crossing Bassett's Creek into the city from the north and west on a single day in 1868, and it was thought that again as many arrived at Bridge Square from other directions.

Another industry was introduced to St. Anthony and Minneapolis in the spring of 1861 when David Lewis, a weaver seeking a climate more healthful than his native Massachusetts, brought in the first elementary textile machinery. A double carding machine and a jack spinner were set up in a shop to do what was called "custom work." Farmers brought wool here to be carded, after which their womenfolk would spin and weave it at home. The carding mill enjoyed a good business.

The next year a Mr. Hilliard brought a loom and spinning machinery from Salisbury, Vermont. One box of the equipment was lost in transit and had to be replaced by makeshift parts made in a shop at Northfield. After great difficulty the machinery was put into operation. It was driven by waterpower and turned out about 60 yards of cloth per day, and it encouraged other establishments in the same field.

Settlers from New England hoped that Minneapolis might sometime rival the great textile centers such as Lawrence and Lowell. Progress was made in that direction, too; in 1865, $100,000 worth of woolen and cotton fabrics were produced.

In 1866 iron works, car and machine shops, three planing mills, a sash and door factory, one paper mill in operation and another about to be opened, furniture factories and other establishments which turned out "articles of luxury as well as of necessity," already gave color to the claim of Minneapolis that she was to be Minnesota's leading industrial city.

It had already become apparent that it would be to the advantage of the two cities at the Falls to unite; for all practical purposes they were already one. Two city governments were being maintained, which was costly and inefficient. On March 18, 1866, a proposal to unite was submitted to the voters and was defeated by the narrow margin of 85 votes. Minneapolis had been forging ahead so rapidly that it was apparent she would absorb her neighbor if they were made one, and St. Anthony was not ready to admit defeat.

One of the dangers about which the early newspapers wrote continually and ominously was fire. If lumber was the financial prop of the cities it was also their building material, for even the business district was constructed almost entirely of wood. These tinder-like buildings and the lack of fire equipment meant that a blaze might wipe out the entire settlement. One editor warned that four things were needed to guarantee the future of the city: "A good public schoolhouse; a strong lock up . . . a fireproof depositary for the records and documents of the Register's office; and a steam fire engine." His plea was unheeded. A jail was regarded as "unnecessary expenditure of public funds" by sedate Minneapolitans, and nothing was done in regard to fire protection.

In consequence, on March 19, 1866, one-third of the business district was destroyed by fire, with a total loss of nearly a hundred thousand dollars. It had been a minor blaze at first, and with proper fire-fighting equipment the damage would have been small, but there was no fire engine and the little hand pump could not function in the sub-zero weather. The citizens were forced to stand by and see building after building catch fire and go down. It was possible to rescue quantities of goods, but it seemed for a time as if all the buildings of the business district must go. Only through heroic effort and the setting of counter-fires was the blaze brought under control. Next day a newspaper reported that "sadness prevailed."

The sadness did not last very long. Now that the ugly early growth was cleared away, a better city soon rose from the ruins. Two hundred and fifty buildings were erected in the next month. Soon the "four requisites" for the future of the city were provided. It was later recorded that one of these, the county jail, was "a most complete and elegant stone structure."

Growth in the 1860's might be measured by the fact that by 1867 fifty-one lawyers had taken out licenses. A local paper recorded the fact under a headline noting that the country was "In An Awful State."

Traffic was already beginning to present a problem. A city ordinance provided that horses might not be driven over six miles an hour, but this law was often broken. One editor explained the temptation that faced drivers: "the sleighing is fine, horses 'feel their oats' and it's a natural desire to 'let them out' . . ." Another impediment to progress and affront to civic pride was that livestock of every variety roamed freely over the streets, until a pound-master "gobbled a drove of them . . . and 'enclosed 'em'," teaching the owners a much needed lesson.

A hall with impressive stage equipment was opened to the public in 1864 at the corner of Washington and Nicollet. It was called Harrison's Hall, and was used for entertainments and public meetings. One of the groups which used the Hall as a forum was the Liberal League, which was said to be "abhorred by the good church people."

Three years later the Pence Opera House was built, and in this building Minneapolis received its full share of genuine theatre, with all the attendant trappings and glamour. To summon the crowd, a band played on an outside balcony. Performances were opened by a gentleman who came before the curtain (itself a remarkable work of art entitled The Vintage Festival) to ignite the footlights with a torch. Several short acts, then known as "curtain warmers," usually preceded the main show.

The people who had come to Minnesota from older and more civilized places were hungry for culture. This was shown from the first in their interest in schools and libraries, and now in their patronage of the theatre, which was so deep and widespread as to bring to the city the best of the drama of that time. In the 1880's Sir Henry Irving, Ellen Terry, Richard Mansfield, Sara Bernhardt, Lillian Russell, and other noted actors played here. It was remarked at the time that the people of Minneapolis could attend the "finest presentations of musical and dramatic offerings that it was possible to obtain in any city of the United States, New York not excepted."

The entire life of the city depended more or less upon the water power at the Falls, and panic almost ensued in 1869 when word spread that the Falls were going out. The excavation of a tunnel through an island to get a greater head of water for power had weakened the limestone ledge, and a section of it collapsed. The frantic people tried to stem the torrent by throwing logs, rock, brush, hay and rubbish into the break, but the force of the current was too strong for such measures. It was soon apparent that this was too vast a calamity to be handled locally, and Washington was petitioned to save the Falls. Engineers were sent out, and in 1870 over a million dollars was spent by the Federal Government in the construction of a concrete barrier to support the ledge and protect the river bed. When men working on the repairs who had been promised $2.50 a day were paid a lesser amount, the result was an unorganized strike. Labor, however, was plentiful, and most of the men returned to work on threat of losing their jobs to others.

Minneapolis labor asserted itself again in the same year. Coopers who were engaged in making barrels for the shipments of flour went on strike, "demanding an extraordinary advance" from 18 to 25 cents per barrel. Some employers compromised immediately, granting a raise of two cents a barrel. Others were more obdurate, and it was at this time that millers began shipping flour in cloth sacks.

Mighty Kingdoms Will Emerge
Minneapolis Reaches Maturity

In 1866 Minneapolis' boundaries had been enlarged to include St. Anthony, but only for certain specified purposes. Some functions of government were combined, but the elder settlement yet retained its identity. St. Anthony was the older and better known of the two cities, and the early settlers had a great deal of local pride. Minneapolis, however, had the larger population, and it was this strength of numbers which eventually resolved the deadlock, when on February 28, 1872, a legislative act consolidated the two cities under the name Minneapolis. The consolidation placed Minneapolis in a better position to compete with St. Paul for immigrants and trade.

Scandinavians, so important later on, had played little part in the early history of Minneapolis. The first Swede to come, a shoemaker by the name of Nils Nyberg, arrived in St. Anthony in 1851 and opened a small shop for the practice of his trade. The first Norwegian, Fredrika Bremer, the famous novelist, came to the settlement in 1850, but merely for a visit; there were no actual Norwegian settlers until 1854. As an unusual event, Mrs. Ard Godfrey recorded in her dairy in 1858: "April 29—Seven Norwegians came to tea. April 30— . . . Norwegians left after dinner. May 5—Norwegians came to dinner again. May 6—They left [yesterday?] after dinner again."

Scandinavian immigration did not assume large proportions until the early 1860's. Until that time the only considerable body of foreigners had been the French-Canadians. Thus the early affairs of the city and its commerce were guided largely by settlers from the eastern states, for whom New England was both inspiration and pattern. The first influx of Scandinavians caused considerable alarm, but later they were recognized as solid and dependable citizens, and more and more, in proportion to their numerical strength, they assumed a leading place in the community.

The language difficulty facing the newcomers created an educational problem which the city met, in the winter of 1871, by establishing a school in a basement, where a one-time Baptist minister instructed young Scandinavians in the English language.

One of the favorite amusements of the seventies and early eighties was Bill King's annual Fair at 27th Avenue South and 24th Street. Here there was a fine race track which brought to Minneapolis the famous trotting horses of the country, and a grandstand and four exhibition buildings, the whole surrounded by an eight-foot unpainted board fence. An imitation Minnehaha Falls "cleverly arranged with no pipes in view" drew large crowds, though the actual Falls were almost as easily accessible. The Fair, which was the only one in the State for a number of years, presented many attractions. One visitor reported that "President Hayes was there during his administration and so were Hopeful and Rarus, leading trotters of the day."

From the Civil War to the early 1870's the foundations of the great railway systems were laid, the cities were consolidated, and industry was stabilized. The "Jay Cooke" panic of 1873 marked the conclusion of an era of "frenzied finance." This panic was almost as widespread as the one in 1857 and had similar effects on Minneapolis. However, the country was not as long recovering from it. Recovery brought with it a period of the most rapid development in population, industry, business and civic improvement.

A street railway line was built in 1875, extending from Fourth Avenue North down to Hennepin and then across the bridge. The horse-drawn cars provided a small coupe in front for the driver, heated by a small stove that threw a minimum of heat to the passengers in the rear. The lines were extended and the company reorganized, with Thomas Lowry, who eventually obtained control, as attorney. Electric cars were first put in operation in 1889, overcoming many difficulties which had made the horse cars a trial to patience and temper. Before the innovation of electric cars, extra horses had to be maintained at the foot of steep hills, to aid the regular Dobbin.

None of the city streets were paved until 1878. The winter of that year was warm, and streets became rivers of sticky mud. One street car actually stood stranded and deserted for several months in a swampy place between Sixth and Eighth Avenues. Out of the experience of that season grew an insistent public demand for paved streets for the preservation of both temper and civic dignity.

Introduction of each new invention or device brought difficulties for the innovators. The telegraph, illuminating gas, the telephone, and later, electricity, each so vitally to affect the future of the community, were at first extremely restricted luxuries, and had to overcome many prejudices before they met with acceptance.

The telephone was introduced in June 1877, when a line was installed from the Hankinson residence, at Sixth Avenue North and Bradford, to the City Hall. The first test was made by the lady of the house singing hymns to her husband at the city hall, and it was remarked that the device "worked very satisfactorily if the party at the other end was quite familiar with the tunes."

[62]

Later a line was put up from the offices of Loring and Fletcher to their mill at Minnetonka Mills, a distance of fifteen miles. Materials were makeshift; the experiment was hardly a success. Mr. Fletcher was constantly annoyed by weird noises on the wire, ranging from "the croaking of frogs, rustling of leaves and barking of dogs to the cry of the banshee." He ordered the telephone company to eliminate these noises, but was informed that his mill was so located that this could not be done. This answer only infuriated Mr. Fletcher, who retorted that the mill would not be moved for any telephone and that unless the company "constructed their line of something besides old hay wire they could take it down." In the next year, the difficulties having been conquered, the Northwestern Telephone Company was organized and a small exchange was established in the old City Hall.

Minneapolis was fortunate to be building itself and its industries during the golden age of invention, so that it need not pass through the tedious and costly process of complete rebuilding when new methods and machines made their appearance. And if natural development did not provide for this, fate sometimes stepped in to clear the stage for the next improvement.

On May 2, 1878, a disaster in the flour industry made way for revolutionary changes in the milling process, which had remained substantially unchanged for centuries. Late on this cloudless day the city was shaken by a terrific explosion. It was some time before the stunned citizens received the news that "the Mills have blown up." A rain of shingles fell over the city and firebrands were carried as far as a mile away from the explosion and resulting fire. South Minneapolis lay in the direction of the wind, and the spread of fire from the burning fragments had to be prevented by chains of men carrying water to the roofs of threatened buildings. For three hours the perilous rain of debris and sparks continued, and despite all efforts to save them, a number of dwellings were destroyed.

The explosion took place in the Washburn A Mill, and the flames spread until five smaller mills, a factory, a machine shop and a roundhouse were destroyed. The cause of the explosion was never definitely determined, but later investigators believed that it was the result of ignition of flour dust. Eighteen men were killed in this disaster. By this time the flour industry had too much vitality to be greatly retarded by the calamity, and plans for rebuilding were immediately made.

The hard, red spring wheat of the plains states, Minnesota, North and South Dakota and Montana, had, until this date, been at a disadvantage in competition with the soft winter wheat of the East and South. There was a great deal of waste in milling, and the dark color of the flour, even though its food value was higher, led people to believe it inferior. Before the explosion, an improvement in milling had already been introduced in the form of a middlings purifier, the invention of Edmund N. La Croix, a French immigrant. This invention saved much of the grain formerly dumped into the river as middlings and wastage, but the dust raised by this process was thought to be responsible for the explosions. The new mills were built with facilities for eliminating the dangerous condition.

In some of these new mills a process was inaugurated which involved a basic change in milling practice. The milling process, from primitive times up to that day, had consisted of grinding the grain between the surfaces of two mill stones. By the new method, the grain was passed through a set of rollers which gradually reduced it to a fine flour, permitting the elimination, without waste, of the outer layers of the kernel. It is these that contain the darkening pigment. By this process, the amount of saleable flour produced from a bushel of grain was increased from 25 to 90 per cent.

The flour which could now be milled from spring wheat was of such quality that it soon captured the markets of the world. Flour was shipped from Minneapolis in increasing quantities, and the capital needed to rebuild and enlarge the mills was readily available. Giant elevators and mills soon began rising in Minneapolis, tokens of its growing supremacy in flour.

The growth of the mills brought more and more wheat to the city, taxing all storage facilities beyond capacity. In 1879 there were elevators for storing about ten million bushels, but this one year brought ten times that quantity rolling in from the prairie. Great elevators had to be built, and these transformed the skyline of the city. At first the grain trade was almost completely controlled by the milling interests, but as the demand for northwest wheat increased, the Minneapolis Chamber of Commerce was organized, in 1882, to carry on that trade.

Since the beginning of the railway era, certain men had been interested in a northern route to the Pacific which would pass through Minnesota. In the East, Minnesota and the Dakotas had been extravagantly advertised as having a mild, warm climate, and when the projected trans-continental northern route was outlined, it was derided as "Jay Gould's Banana Belt." Progress on this railway was inexplicably slow, and when the work threatened to go completely under, financial reverses forced a sweeping reorganization of the company. Eventually, in November 1883, the Northern Pacific was completed. Since it meant a vast new extension of trade for Minneapolis, it was greeted with rejoicing. Henry Villard, president of the line, was met as he passed through the city by a mammoth parade headed by a huge model of a flour mill, symbol of Minneapolis prosperity.

Unlike most frontier settlements and boom towns, early Minneapolis had been characterized by staidness and respectability. The New Englanders who dominated the life of the city preached, and practiced, a high moral standard. It was hard for them to understand the gayety and roughness of the men who came later: the lumberjacks, the foreigners, people who sought relief from the daily monotony of life.

On the western side of Minneapolis, Kegan Lake, where the Westphal Brewery had been built, became, in the Eighties, a popular resort. It lay outside the restrictions of the city, and high carnival was held there on warm Sunday afternoons. There was a small park around the brewery, and near it was a dance hall and bar where, it was reported with shocked disgust, "prize fights were often pulled off." As the city spread out, it absorbed this area, the gay scenes disappeared, and the brewery closed down.

Minneapolis, growing in industrial importance, felt the need for an Exposition which would acquaint the public at large with the diversity and importance of its products. The outdoor fairs were devoted almost exclusively to agriculture, and most of them had not been successful. A movement for the construction of an Industrial Exposition Building was initiated in September 1885, and business, civic and labor groups participated in a drive to finance such a project. The site of the old Winslow House was chosen; and the building, which had been closed, re-opened as Macalester College, and now again stood empty, was torn down to give way to the new structure. On August 23, 1886, Mrs. Grover Cleveland opened the building by remote control from upper Saranac Lake, where she and the President were vacationing. Despite great expectations, however, the Exposition operated at a consistent loss, its sponsors were forced to withdraw, and it closed in 1891.

The next year, however, the city felt that it had received the crown of national acclaim when the Republicans decided upon it as their national convention city. This not only meant thousands of dollars in additional trade from convention visitors; it also meant that people from the most remote sections of the nation would be made aware of the possibilities of Minneapolis.

That convention, in June of 1892, brought the largest influx of visitors that the city had ever seen. The new West Hotel, which had already won distinction, was thronged with important looking men. Crowds of people waited on the streets to catch a glimpse of national Republican leaders such as the rising young Governor of Ohio, William McKinley.

On the eve of the convention a public meeting was held to dedicate the redecorated Exposition building, which had been fitted up as an auditorium. The great hall was impressive in blue and gold, climaxed by a skylight of "soft blue studded with stars of white." The dedicatory program, which featured the appearance of a thousand-voiced chorus and the "golden tongued" Chauncey Depew, packed the place with a richly dressed crowd which inspired one newspaper to report that "no far famed vale of Vallambrosa was more thickly strewn with autumn leaves than the . . . hall was gemmed last night with the fairest and bravest of the country. All other occasions in the history of this city pall into insignificance." Perhaps the reporter erred on the side of enthusiasm, but the event did have one lasting influence in that it made the city convention-minded.

Labor had grown more and more aggressive since the organization of the first actual trade union by the printers in 1859. In 1889 the first large-scale organized strike occurred, when the streetcar workers walked out on April 11, following the posting of a notice by Mr. Lowry, head of the street transportation company, to the effect that wages would be reduced to 15 and 17 cents per hour. He also had demanded that all men employed by him sign an "iron clad," a written promise to stay out of labor organizations on pain of discharge. The public, although much inconvenienced, supported the action of workers. Some violence resulted when an attempt was made to run the cars with men brought in from other cities. The strike was finally settled with a partial compromise, after a long period in which the management refused to arbitrate.

After the consolidation of St. Anthony and Minneapolis, St. Paul had but one rival, and that a greatly strengthened one. Consequently the bitter wrangling between the cities broke out anew. The newspapers, particularly, were continually fanning the flames of discord. A St. Paul editor would refer to Minneapolis building reports as "fictitious," and in retaliation Minneapolitans would be warned that "strangers coming to St. Paul are particularly cautioned to avoid that part of the city where sidewalks are usually found. They have been torn up about every twenty yards to give the city a business look and prevent strangers from thinking that the town is finished and fenced in."

As Minneapolis' population figures soared nearer and nearer the mark set by St. Paul (no one knew just when Minneapolis passed her sister city), there was constant bickering on the question of population. Every census brought renewed and vociferous mutual charges of "puffing" and "padding" figures. The census of 1880 revealed that Minneapolis had overtaken St. Paul, even though that city had, according to Minneapolitans, "invented new and novel ways of securing names on a comprehensive scale." Minneapolis excused its own errors by claiming that in "rapidly growing America, especially in the hustling, bustling western states, many anomalies necessarily appear." St. Paul then attempted to minimize the more rapid growth of Minneapolis by talk of the two cities being equal, which antagonistic persons characterized as a "ridiculous attempt" to do the "twin sister act."

The census of 1890 brought the dispute to a climax. Minneapolis enumerators were working late on the evening of June 17 when a U. S. Deputy Marshall arrived, arrested seven on charges of fraud and confiscated the census tabulations. Indignant Minneapolis citizens rushed a train to St. Paul with bail funds and succeeded in getting the prisoners released. Next day Minneapolis papers declared in bold face that "IT MEANS WAR," and leading citizens voiced angry threats. Mayor W. H. Eustis was sent with a party of citizens to reclaim the records, and was repulsed by policemen with drawn revolvers who were said to have kicked the good mayor "at least sixteen feet."

This was too much, and Minneapolis began to demand the removal of the capitol from St. Paul. St. Paul then became indignant, and publicly regretted its forced connection with a city "that stands degraded and ashamed in the eyes of the nation." Investigators found the whole census a frightful tangle and a new one was taken. An honest count revealed that neither city had clean hands; in Minneapolis the dead had been enrolled in the interest of civic pride, while St. Paul's standing had been defended by hundreds of inhabitants who evidently lived in depots, barber shops and dime museums. Minneapolis, though proven the more adept at padding figures, was also found to have won by a safe margin, 164,738 to 133,156. This lead has since been maintained and increased.

Shortly following this triumph, however, business began to slow down, and in the 1893 panic which swept the nation, Minneapolis' boasted 38 millionaires were considerably reduced in number, and there was genuine poverty among the working people. It was several years before any real recovery was apparent.

When it came, lumber production was still increasing at an amazing rate, although men had begun to notice a thinning of the supposedly boundless forests. The zenith of the lumber industry was reached in 1899, with a production of 594 million feet. This was the last big haul. The industry began then to move westward to a source of greater supply, the forests of the Pacific slope. In 1900, Minneapolis was still one of the nation's chief lumber centers, but the years following were marked by decline. From 1910 production figures plunged downward like a spent rocket, and in 1919 with the closing of the last mill, the first great industry of the city passed out of existence. Lumber had performed its role, furnishing the impetus and the capital from which arose new industries and occupations.

It may have been a portent that the first permanent settler in Minneapolis proper was a farmer. The military men, the grasping, rapacious Indian traders, the speculators, all looked with disdain on the efforts of humble men who sought to wring their living from the land. Yet it was hard labor on the land which, in the end, provided the real economic foundation of the Northwest.

Agriculture, and the industries based upon it, moved steadily forward. The decade of 1870 to 1880 brought a rapid increase in the amount of wheat grown in the trade territory. This wheat flowed towards Minneapolis and in a short time made the city one of the most important primary wheat markets. By 1885 Minneapolis led the world in flour production.

Around the flour mills new industries developed, and the network of commerce which connected Minneapolis with the farm country of the Northwest strengthened. Grain companies, naturally centering their activities in Minneapolis, began to extend chains of elevators to the little sidings on the prairies where farmers delivered their grain, and of course, as the farm economy of the Northwest came to center ever more directly in Minneapolis, it had to follow that the surrounding region found itself depending more and more upon that city to supply its financial needs and banking facilities.

Wheat, because of the ease with which it was stored and shipped, was the favorite crop of Northwest farmers. As storage and transportation facilities improved, however, they began to raise other grains. Quantities of oats and corn were being sent to Minneapolis before 1890. Nineteen hundred saw Minneapolis established as one of the country's leading flax markets, and by 1905 it was a major market for barley and rye. Chicago remained the largest all-grain market, but Minneapolis was at times a potentially dangerous rival.

Jobbing and wholesaling soon felt the influence of this growing trade in grain. In a period of ten years, between 1880 and 1890, Minneapolis, climbing in spectacular leaps, overtook and surpassed the once commanding lead which St. Paul had enjoyed as a jobbing center. Successive panics produced temporary setbacks, but the general trend was sharply upward, until by 1919 Minneapolis was able to call herself the "billion dollar market." Nor was it just an idle, vainglorious claim; concrete evidence of its truth was to be seen in the rush of large eastern wholesalers to set up branches in the new trade center.

The city in this period also became prominent as a labor market. Skilled building tradesmen, lumberjacks, and railroad workers were among the early labor needs supplied. Minneapolis was peculiarly suited for this service—there was lumbering and mining to the north, railroads were reaching out in all directions, and farmers to the south and west were demanding helpers. By the early 1920's the supplying of labor to surrounding areas and states had become an important function of the city.

After the turn of the century, Minneapolis entered decisively into the financial stage of its development. The area over which it began to exercise financial control was substantially the same as that it had served in marketing and manufacturing. The wealth of the entire region tended to concentrate in the city, so that its stake in agriculture was even greater than it had been when the city was dependent upon the farms merely for supplies.

Organization in 1914 of the Ninth Federal Reserve District, with headquarters in Minneapolis, and embracing Montana, North Dakota, South Dakota, Minnesota, the northern peninsula of Michigan and the northern two-thirds of Wisconsin, merely marked the official recognition of an already established fact. For some years, the city had been dominant in Northwest finance. It was designated as reserve district headquarters after Minneapolis business groups had organized and presented conclusive proof of the city's financial leadership to the Reserve Bank Organization Committee.

Since those days, of course, drastic changes have taken place in the banking structure of the Northwest. At one time there were 3,782 banks in the Ninth Federal Reserve District. By 1927, bank casualties resulting in the main from depressed agricultural prices had reduced the number to 2,613; in mid-1939, only 1,312 of these were still in operation. These figures, if taken by themselves, would seem to indicate a sharp decline in the banking resources of this area, with a proportionate reduction in the financial influence that centers in Minneapolis. Such, however, is not the case.

Two factors account for the reduction in number of banks. The rising curve of bank failures from early in the twenties until the bank holiday was proclaimed in 1933 does represent an actual crippling of the region's financial structure. The other factor accounting for the decrease in number of banks is a long series of mergers and consolidations which actually brought new strength to the general structure. This is illustrated graphically in the fact that the 2,613 banks operating in the Minneapolis district in 1927 had approximately 1,700 million dollars in total deposits, while in 1939, although the number of banks had then dropped to 1,312 the deposit total still stood at 1,429 millions.

This tendency toward centralization of banking control was especially apparent in Minneapolis itself. In the early 1920's some of the younger bankers decided it would promote financial stability to gather the strong outlying banks together into a central corporation. This developed into the group banking system, of which Minneapolis is still a leading exponent. Two large group systems now have headquarters in Minneapolis, one of which concentrates the resources of 80 banks and three branches, the other of 85 banks and 21 branches or offices. By 1937 annual bank clearings in Minneapolis were more than three billion dollars, while at the beginning of 1940, total deposits in the city's banks touched the all-time peak of $402,909,000. By reason of its growing financial power, the city is in a sense no longer dependent on but dominant over the surrounding region.

World War prices brought unprecedented prosperity to agriculture, and millions of acres of previously unused land were placed under the plow. Europe hungered for wheat, and more and more of it passed through the Minneapolis terminal. When the war ended and Europe returned to production, world markets were soon glutted. The ensuing sharp decline in export trade struck Minneapolis the first of a series of blows.

The official opening of the Panama Canal on July 12, 1920,* marked the beginning of a new adversity. East-west transcontinental shipping was seriously curtailed, and this reduced the importance of Minneapolis as a central point in cross-country shipping.

In addition to these reverses, the flour and grain market of Minneapolis suffered from an Interstate Commerce Commission ruling on freight rates, of February 14, 1922, to the effect that "water competition on the Upper Mississippi, north of St. Louis, is no longer recognized as a controlling force, but is little more than potential." This decision greatly increased the freight rates of the area, so that annual average grain receipts at Minneapolis suffered a drop of over 25 million bushels, while flour production declined to less than eight million barrels yearly.

In 1925 it was still said that "the city's position as chief flour-producing center has not been seriously threatened by any other city in the country." However, since it was cheaper to ship wheat than flour, milling centers began to grow up in other sections of the country, either closer to the source of supply or in places not affected by adverse freight rates. Like the lumber barons before them, the milling interests simply transferred their activities. Minneapolis money still controls 85 per cent of Buffalo milling, 25 per cent in Kansas City, and many mills elsewhere. Buffalo, since 1929, has surpassed Minneapolis in flour production by nearly two million barrels per year.

Despite these setbacks the twenties were a fantastically opulent decade. The old families, the New Englanders who had made fortunes in lumber and flour and grain, were now able to sit back and enjoy their imperial city. Minneapolis began for the first time to display its wealth. The wealthy families, taking advantage of the new mobility of the automobile age, moved towards the edge of the city on Lake Harriet and Lake of the Isles or even outside the city to Lake Minnetonka. Nicollet Avenue became one of the finest shopping districts in the country. A new generation in the city's business life outlined structures and projects which would imbed

* The Panama Canal was opened to allow the steamer *Ancon* passage on August 15, 1914 and was formally opened by President Theodore Roosevelt on July 12, 1915. Traffic in the early years was hampered by slides and reduced by war conditions. It was officially opened five years after its formal opening.

[70]

their names as securely in the future city as the milling and lumber men had done before them.

In 1927 the three million dollar Municipal Auditorium was completed, work was begun on the Foshay Tower and the Sears, Roebuck plant. That single year saw building permits issued for a total of 22 million dollars worth of construction. Twenty-five new industries found a place in the city during the year. It was confidently expected that building in 1928 would exceed 25 million dollars in cost. The Calhoun Beach Club, still uncompleted in 1940, was then under construction, and a new advance in industry was anticipated.

Minneapolis failed to notice the exact point at which it outgrew the Northwest. There was always a surplus of jobless men on the Minneapolis market, and cheap labor became the accepted standard. This cheap labor attracted new industries, metal, linseed oil, clothing and knitting. These additions compensated for the decline in flour production. Expansion was the accepted creed of the day.

Diversification proved to be a temporary answer to the industrial problems of the city. Whereas in 1868 the important industries were lumber, flour, iron and metal products, wood products and woolen goods, by 1929 the list had already come to include mill products, printing and publishing, foundry products, bread and bakery goods, rail car construction and repair, prepared animal feeds, electrical equipment, furniture, butter, coffee and spices. The decline of wheat led to a similar diversification in agriculture, and as a result Minneapolis assumed importance as a poultry and dairy center.

The height of postwar prosperity was reached in 1927, and the new buildings that were rising high over the business district were symbols of this grandiose epoch. Most striking of these was the obelisk-like Foshay Tower, inspired by the Washington Monument. It was said at the time of its completion that: "Paris has its Eiffel Tower and the Louvre; London, Westminster Abbey; New York, the Statue of Liberty; Washington, the White House; and now Minneapolis has the Foshay Tower. . . It is possible because Mr. Foshay had faith in the future of Minneapolis and the Northwest and because he had the fortitude and daring and vision to use that faith."

A few years later, the era of "faith" had come to an end, the Foshay utilities scheme, with many others of its kind, lay in ruins, and Minneapolis was feeling the overwhelming panic which followed the crisis of 1929. Unemployment soon reached new heights, and as it rose the labor problem grew more acute.

The distance traveled in those catastrophic years might be gauged by the span from the magnificence of the Foshay Tower to the woebegone misery of Bridge Square. The Square, once the most prosperous business section of Minneapolis, now a tumbledown collection of cheap movie houses, penny restaurants, squalid "flop joints," penny arcades and pawnshops, revealed the problem clearly, for it was and is peopled by Minnesota's past. Each industry that has declined, or come to an end, left behind a share of despondent human backwash. The Square had once been a labor market for the farms and pineries; now, its only product unwanted, it became a place of idle men and aimless despair.

Wilbur Foshay's fall had been a shock to Minneapolis, but it was not as severe as that which resulted from the collapse of the Backus fortune, rooted in lumber and paper. E. W. Backus was one of the old, well established generation of eastern origin whose history is inextricably woven into that of the city. His bankruptcy in 1931 shook the city and ended an era.

The new era opened rather unpropitiously with the truck drivers' strike of May 1934. Minneapolis was still a cheap labor area, but the rising cost of living turned employed workers more and more to self-organization as an answer to their problems. The truck drivers' strike was successful, and as a result unionization of Minneapolis labor spread rapidly and with less opposition. This strike forced Minneapolis to consider her industrial problems realistically.

The immediate problems were partially alleviated by the reform policies of the Roosevelt Administration. Various relief methods were tried, among them the Works Progress Administration (now the Work Projects Administration) for the purpose of making public improvements and rendering public service through use and preservation of the skills possessed by the unemployed.

Present day Minneapolis is less ebullient than it was during the day of the "booster" in the twenties; yet it is optimistic. Today's realism finds new reasons to be hopeful for the future of Minneapolis and the Northwest.

There is considerable hope that the "potential" of river traffic will be revived and thus bring about a lowering of unfavorable railroad rates. The renewed effort to revive river traffic was opened by the arrival of the first modern tow boat on August 25, 1927. It may be that the future outlet for a share of the Northwest's agricultural products will be down the Mississippi to southern ports and perhaps to Latin America.

The financial crisis, although severe, did not strike the city with the deadening force which it exerted in some sections of the country. It was cushioned and delayed by the fact that diversification had already entered the farming and industrial picture in this area. Progress towards recovery was more rapid for the same reason. The city's interest in agriculture provided a stable base for both industry and finance. The high percentage of home owners found in Minneapolis testifies to this stability.

Industry is contriving through constant diversification to fit itself ever more closely to the supply and employment needs of the area. The number of manufacturing establishments increased from 923 in 1933 to 1,100 in 1939. The three largest manufacturing firms make agricultural implements, thermostats for heating apparatus, and underwear.

Culturally the city is in an enviable position. Its institutional framework, erected upon the foundations so soundly laid by the early settlers, are of the nature and scope which may be expected to provide the finest and most varied cultural opportunities. It is significant that the past decade has witnessed a broadening of the appreciation and enjoyment of these facilities. Modern wealth travels and can afford to seek education and enjoyment in the largest metropolitan centers. Consequently its support of civic culture, in some cases, has declined. The result, surely not an unhappy one, has been to broaden the basis of support for and participation in cultural institutions among all groups of people, rather than leave the burden of support entirely to a wealthy few.

Most Minneapolitans express pride in the local educational system, the Minneapolis Symphony Orchestra, and the city's position as an art center. Facts more than justify this pride. The origins of the Minneapolis Symphony extend deep into the city's past. As far back as 1866 a visiting composer remarked that he found "voices remarkably clear, pure and healthy . . . the pure, dry, invigorating climate of your state cannot but be favorable to vocal development . . . Instrumental musical talent is also well represented, and is evidently encouraged here. . . ." During the same year a local newspaper speculated on the city's musical future; "Who knows but in time we may have an opera established here. Stranger things have happened."

Minneapolis didn't get an opera, but its symphony orchestra has an international reputation. The orchestra, a genuinely civic product, grew logically out of the small orchestras of the early days, the Danz Orchestra of the eighties and the Philharmonix of the nineties, and has been in continuous existence since that time. To the first conductor, Emil Oberhoffer, must go primary credit for the stable orchestra organization. Henri Verbrugghen became conductor in 1922, and Eugene Ormandy, now co-conductor of the Philadelphia Symphony Orchestra, succeeded him in 1931. Dimitri Mitropolous, the present conductor, succeeded Ormandy in 1936. The artistic growth of the organization has been consistent and recently has encouraged the development of Minnesota composers, notably John Verrall.

The Walker Art Galleries, containing the collected paintings, ceramics and jade of the millionaire lumberman, T. B. Walker, was re-opened in

January 1940, as the Walker Art Center. Under the sponsorship of the Minnesota Arts Council and with the cooperation of the Minnesota Art Project, Work Projects Administration, the new center is expected to increase popular enjoyment and participation in the arts. The Minneapolis Institute of Art, also known for its outstanding collection of ceramics and jade, continues to play an outstanding role in extending art appreciation. The Institute has a professional art school which enjoys a high rating.

The University of Minnesota, located in Minneapolis, is second in the United States in number of students enrolled. The University takes more pride, however, in the high academic standing of its component schools and colleges than in its size, although the total enrollment does indicate the intense desire for higher education which is found in Minneapolis and Minnesota.

The comprehensive system of public instruction, under the direction of the Minneapolis Board of Education, includes six senior high schools, three junior-senior high schools, 13 junior high scools, one boys' vocational school, one girls' vocational school, 88 grade schools and two special schools and special classes for deaf students. Wise and careful management has kept Minneapolis schools open even during the worst years of the depression.

The completion of the first hundred years of Minneapolis progress was celebrated in October 1939. The new century holds many problems. Although the city yet dominates the Northwest's agricultural empire, it faces a period of readjustment to a changing world. Rival social forces active within its population challenge each other for leadership—each hoping to control and guide the future destiny of the city.

Conflicts such as this are not peculiar to Minneapolis; they exist today in all large population centers. The careful student of Minneapolis history can view them calmly and without foreboding, for he knows what the city has done in the past. He knows it has faced, in its first hundred years, many other situations which at the time seemed equally as difficult. He knows that these problems have always been met full face, with daring and ingenuity, and that a stronger, more closely knit community has emerged out of the conflict. So long as that spirit endures, recurrent problems will be solved, and Minneapolis will continue to thrive.

OLD FORT SNELLING, ABOUT 1845

MINNEAPOLIS IN 1940

OLD GOVERNMENT FLOUR MILL

MINNEHAHA FALLS IN 1867

STEAMBOAT MINNEAPOLIS, 1869

FIRST SUSPENSION BRIDGE

ST. ANTHONY AND MINNEAPOLIS IN 1857

HENNEPIN AVENUE IN 1869

ST. PAUL AND PACIFIC RAILWAY DEPOT, 1874

THE FIRST REAL ESTATE OFFICE, ABOUT 1856

A HOME IN THE SEVENTIES

OLD MAIN, UNIVERSITY OF MINNESOTA. ABOUT 1886

THE NICOLLET HOUSE IN THE SEVENTIES

REPUBLICAN NATIONAL CONVENTION, 1892

AT THE CITY MARKET, 1900

STREET SCENE, 1890

Notes on Illustrations

OLD FORT SNELLING, ABOUT 1845

Reproduced from the painting by Seth Eastman, commandant at Fort Snelling during parts of the period 1841-48, who painted a number of pictures of Minnesota in romantic style. The picture is here reproduced through the courtesy of Julius H. Weitzner, Inc., 36 East 57th St., New York City.

MINNEAPOLIS IN 1940

Skyline of the city's business district from Loring Park. Photograph by Norton & Peel. Courtesy of the Minneapolis Civic & Commerce Association.

OLD GOVERNMENT FLOUR MILL

This photograph of the Government Flour Mill erected on the banks of the Mississippi in 1822 was taken in 1857, and published by Edward Augustus Bromley (1848-1925) from the original Benjamin Franklin Upton negatives. To Upton, frontier photographer who left Minneapolis in the 70's to live in Florida, and Bromley, photographer and collector, the city is indebted for many of the pictures that document its history. Courtesy of the Minnesota Historical Society.

MINNEHAHA FALLS IN 1867

This picture by an unknown photographer is dated 1867. Courtesy of the Minneapolis Public Library.

STEAMBOAT *Minneapolis*, 1869

The Washington Avenue bridge is on the site of the landing where this riverboat is drawn up. Photographer unknown. Courtesy of the Minneapolis Public Library.

FIRST SUSPENSION BRIDGE

Date of this photograph, possibly by Upton, is uncertain. The first suspension bridge was opened July 4, 1855, and replaced in 1875. Courtesy of the Minneapolis Public Library.

ST. ANTHONY AND MINNEAPOLIS IN 1857

This photograph, taken from the roof of the Winslow House, is No. 5 of a series of eight pictures published by Bromley from the original Upton negatives. Courtesy of the Minnesota Historical Society.

HENNEPIN AVENUE IN 1869

Hennepin Avenue from Washington Avenue towards the river, and the Pence Opera House. Sweet-Jacoby negative. Courtesy of the Minnesota Historical Society.

ST. PAUL AND PACIFIC RAILWAY DEPOT, 1874
The passenger and freight depot, the photograph of which is dated 1874, was located at Washington Avenue and Fourth Avenue North. Photographer unknown. Courtesy of the Minnesota Historical Society.

THE FIRST REAL ESTATE OFFICE, ABOUT 1856
This picture is said to have been taken by Upton in 1856. Snyder and McFarlane's real estate and banking office is supposed to have been the first real estate office opened (1855) "on north side of Bridge Square near old Suspension bridge" in Minneapolis. The men in the picture have been identified as, left to right: Dr. Gilbert, S. P. Snyder, (unknown), J. G. McFarlane, Wm. McFarlane, and W. P. Ankeny. Courtesy of the Minnesota Historical Society.

A HOME IN THE SEVENTIES
This particular home is "Guilford Place, Residence of R. J. Mendenhall," a broker; the house was located on Nicollet avenue at about 18th street. Homes of this type were not uncommon when land and lumber were cheaper than they are today. The original picture appeared in *Illustrated Historical Atlas of the State of Minnesota*, published in 1874, by A. T. Andreas, Chicago. Courtesy of the Minneapolis Public Library.

OLD MAIN, UNIVERSITY OF MINNESOTA, ABOUT 1886
The original picture appeared in a souvenir *Minneapolis Album*, a book of pictures "Published and Copyrighted, 1886, by Adolph Willemann, 25 Park Place, New York," and printed in Leipzig, Germany. Courtesy of the Minnesota Historical Society.

THE NICOLLET HOUSE IN THE SEVENTIES
The original picture appeared in *Illustrated Historical Atlas of the State of Minnesota*. Courtesy of the Minneapolis Public Library.

REPUBLICAN NATIONAL CONVENTION, 1892
This picture of the famous convention held in the old Exposition Building, during June, 1892, is reproduced from a drawing "by F. V. Dumond after a sketch by T. Dart Walker," which appeared in *Harper's Weekly*, June 18, 1892. Courtesy of Harper and Brothers.

AT THE CITY MARKET, 1900
The photographer of this appealing scene is unknown. Courtesy of the Minneapolis Public Library.

STREET SCENE, 1890
This photograph from the E. A. Bromley collection is labeled: "Old Market House, First St. No. and Hennepin Ave. 1890—Bridge Square Gale's Corner." The policeman has been identified as Capt. Qualey, and the man next to him as Harlow A. Gale. Courtesy of the Minneapolis Public Library.

SUGGESTED READING

EARLY EXPLORATION
Folwell, William W., *A History of Minnesota,* Vol. I, Minnesota Historical Society, St. Paul, 1921.

FORT SNELLING
Hansen, Marcus L., *Old Fort Snelling, 1819-1858,* State Historical Society of Iowa, Iowa City, 1918.

ST. ANTHONY AND EARLY MINNEAPOLIS
Atwater, Isaac, *History of the City of Minneapolis,* Munsell and Co., New York, 1893.

Leonard, Dr. William E., "Early Days in Minneapolis," *Minnesota Historical Collections,* Vol. 15, Minnesota Historical Society, St. Paul, 1915.

Stevens, John H., *Recollections of Minnesota and Its People,* Tribune Job Printing Company, Minneapolis, 1890.

MINNEAPOLIS, BUSINESS DEVELOPMENT
Hartsough, Mildred L., *The Twin Cities as a Metropolitan Market,* University of Minnesota Press, Minneapolis, 1925.

MINNEAPOLIS, SOCIAL TRENDS
Schmid, Calvin F., *Social Saga of Two Cities,* Minneapolis Council of Social Agencies, Minneapolis, 1937.

BIBLIOGRAPHY

The following bibliography is a partial list of books, articles and manuscripts consulted in preparation of this volume. There were, in addition, innumerable newspaper items consulted and a number of personal interviews. It was considered necessary to omit the several hundred footnotes of the original manuscript, but completely annotated manuscripts of this history may be consulted at the Minnesota Writers' Project and at the Minnesota Historical Society.

AUTOBIOGRAPHIES, MEMOIRS, AND REMINISCENCES
"Auto-Biography of Major Lawrence Taliaferro," *Minnesota Historical Collections,* Volume 6, St. Paul, 1894.

Bliss, John, "Reminiscences of Fort Snelling," *Minnesota Historical Collections,* Volume 6, St. Paul, 1894.

Coolbaugh, Frank C., "Reminiscences of the Early Days in Minnesota, 1851 to 1861," *Minnesota Historical Collections,* Vol. 15, St. Paul, 1915.

Dick, Helen Dunlap, "A Newly Discovered Diary of Colonel Snelling," *Minnesota History,* Vol. 18, No. 4, December, 1937.

Forsyth, Thomas, "Fort Snelling, Colonel Leavenworth's Expedition to Establish It in 1819," *Minnesota Historical Collection,* Vol. 3, St. Paul, 1880.

Godfrey, Harriet Razada, "Diary of the First White Child Born in Minneapolis," *Minneapolis Journal,* February 20, 1927.

Hale, Mary Thayer, *Early Minneapolis,* privately printed, Minneapolis, 1937.

Leonard, William E., "Early Days in Minneapolis," *Minnesota Historical Collections,* Volume 15, 1915.

Newson, Mary J., "Memories of Fort Snelling in Civil War Days," *Minnesota History,* Volume 15, No. 4, December 1934.

Sibley, Henry H., "Reminiscences, Personal and Historical," *Minnesota Historical Collections,* Volume 1, St. Paul Reprint 1872.

Stevens, John H., *Recollections of Minnesota and Its People,* Tribune Job Printing Co., Minneapolis, 1890.

Ueland, Andreas, *Recollections of an Immigrant,* Minton, Balch Company, New York, 1929.

Van Cleve, Charlotte O., *Three Score Years and Ten,* Harrison & Smith, Minneapolis, 1888.

Walker, Thomas B., "Memories of Early Life and Development of Minnesota," *Minnesota Historical Collections,* Vol. 15, 1915.

Williams, J. Fletcher, "Reminiscences of Mrs. Anne Adams," *Minnesota Historical Collection,* Vol. 6, St. Paul, 1894.

MISCELLANEOUS BOOKS AND PAMPHLETS

Atwater, Isaac, *History of the City of Minneapolis,* Munsell and Company, New York, 1893.

Bisbee, Herman, *Memoir of The Reverend Seth Barnes,* Williamson and Cantwell, Cincinnati, 1868.

Folwell, William Watts, *A History of Minnesota,* Minnesota Historical Society, Vol. 1, St. Paul, 1922.

Gay, Eva, *A Tale of Twin Cities,* Thomas A. Clark Press, Minneapolis, 1889.

Hartsough, Mildred L., *From Canoe to Steel Barge on the Upper Mississippi,* University of Minnesota Press, Minneapolis, 1934.

Hartsough, Mildred L., *The Twin Cities as a Metropolitan Market*, University of Minnesota Press, Minneapolis, 1925.

Hudson, Horace B., *A Half Century of Minneapolis*, Hudson Publishing Company, Minneapolis, 1908.

Johnson, C. W. (comp.), *A Tale of Two Cities, Minneapolis and St. Paul Compared*, Johnson, Smith and Harrison, Minneapolis, 1885.

Lyman, George D., *John Marsh, A Pioneer on Six Borders*, Charles Scribner's Sons, New York, 1930.

Minnesota in The Civil and Indian Wars, 1861-1865, State of Minnesota, St. Paul, 1891.

Neill, Edward D., and Williams, J. Fletcher, *History of Hennepin County and The City of Minneapolis*, North Star Publishing Co., Minneapolis, 1881.

Newson, T. M., *Pen Pictures of St. Paul and Biographical Sketches of Old Settlers*, Published by the Author, St. Paul, 1886.

Parsons, E. Dudley, *The Story of Minneapolis*, Published by the Author, Minneapolis, 1913.

Petersen, William J., *Steamboating on the Upper Mississippi, The Water Way to Iowa*, Iowa Historical Society, Iowa City, 1937.

Potter, Merle C., *101 Best Stories of Minnesota*, Harrison and Smith, Minneapolis, 1931.

Schmid, Calvin F., *Social Saga of Two Cities*, Minneapolis Council of Social Agencies, Minneapolis, 1937.

Shutter, Marion D., *History of Minneapolis*, Vol. 1, S. J. Clarke Publishing Company, Minneapolis and Chicago, 1923.

Steffens, Lincoln, *The Shame of the Cities*, McClure, Philips & Co., New York, 1904.

Thompson, Ruth, *The Twin Towns at the Falls of St. Anthony*, Colwell Press, Minneapolis, 1926.

West, Nathaniel, *The Ancestry, Life and Times of Hon. Henry Hastings Sibley*, Pioneer Press Publishing Company, St. Paul, 1889.

ARTICLES

Baker, James H., "Address at Fort Snelling in the Celebration of the Centennial Anniversary of the Treaty of Pike With the Sioux," *Minnesota Historical Collections*, Volume 12, St. Paul, 1908.

Baker, James H., "A History of Transportation in Minnesota," *Minnesota Historical Collections*, Volume 9, St. Paul, 1901.

Blegen, Theodore C., "The Pond Brothers," *Minnesota History*, Volume 15, No. 4, September 1934.

Bromley, Edward A., "Old Government Mills at the Falls of St. Anthony," *Minnesota Historical Collections*, Vol. 10, Part 2, St. Paul, 1908.

"Early Days at Fort Snelling," *Minnesota Historical Collections,* Vol. 1, St. Paul, Reprint 1872.
Edsall, Samuel Cook, "Reverend Ezekiel Gear, D.D., Chaplain at Fort Snelling," *Minnesota Historical Collections,* Vol. 12, St. Paul, 1908.
Flanagan, John T., "Captain Marryat at Old St. Peters," *Minnesota History,* Volume 18, No. 2, June 1937.
Heilbron, Bertha L., "Christmas and New Years on the Frontier," *Minnesota History,* Vol. 16, No. 4, December 1935.
Hicks, John D., "The Organization of the Volunteer Army in 1861, With Special Reference to Minnesota," *Minnesota History Bulletin,* February, 1918.
Johnson, Richard W., "Fort Snelling From Its Foundation to the Present Time," *Minnesota Historical Collections,* Vol. 8, St. Paul, 1898.
Neill, E. D., "Occurrences in and Around Fort Snelling," *Minnesota Historical Collections,* Volume 2, St. Paul, Reprint 1889.
Rogers, George D., "History of Flour Manufacture in Minnesota," *Minnesota Historical Collections,* Volume 10, Part 1, St. Paul, 1905.
Stanchfield, Daniel, "History of Pioneer Lumbering on the Upper Mississippi and Its Tributaries, With Biographic Sketches," *Minnesota Historical Collections,* Volume 9, St. Paul, 1901.
Woodhall, Allen E., "William Joseph Snelling," *Minnesota History,* Volume 7, No. 3, September 1926.

MANUSCRIPTS

Gyllstrom, Paul, *Notes on Early Minneapolis,* manuscript, Manuscript Division, Minnesota Historical Society.
Hennepin County Historical and Old Settlers Association, *Proceedings, 1867-1871,* bound manuscript volume, Minneapolis Public Library.

NEWSPAPERS

WEEKLY

Minnesota Democrat, (St. Paul) "More New Mills," "The Minnesota University," June 17, 1851.
St. Anthony Express, 1860.
State Atlas (Minneapolis and St. Anthony), 1865.
St. Paul Pioneer and Democrat, 1857-1858.

DAILY

Daily Democrat (St. Paul), "The Rise and Progress of St. Paul," October 28, 1854.
Daily Minnesotian (St. Paul), 1854-1858.
Minneapolis Journal, 1923-1927.
Minneapolis Tribune, 1867-1900.
St. Anthony Falls Evening News, 1860.
St. Paul Daily Pioneer, 1865-1868.
St. Paul Daily Press, 1866.

INDEX

Accault, Michael, 9
Abolitionists, convention of. 52
Adasville, 46
Agriculture, 68, 72; at Fort St. Anthony, 13; first agriculturists, 14; Indians in, 19; growth of, 40, 43; after Civil War, 55; at Minneapolis, 44, 47; export of agricultural products, 57. *See also* Livetock; Hennepin County Agricultural Society
Agricultural Products, importation of, 40; export of, 57; Northwest wheat at disadvantage, 63; wheat as leading Northwest crop, 68
Albion, 46
All Saints, 44, 46
American Board of Foreign Missions, 20
American Fur Company, 17, 29; conflict with Taliaferro, 23; store in St. Anthony, 34
Ames, Albert Alonzo, 24
Ames, Alfred Elisha, 24, 45, 47
Ames, Rev. C. G., 52
Angell, Henry, 30
Anthony, Wayne, steamboat, 37
Ariel, steamboat, 22
Astor, John Jacob, 17
Athenaeum, 53
Atwater, Judge Isaac, 39
Auguelle, Antoine, 9

Bachus, Electa, 33
Babbitt, W. D., 52
Backus, E. W., 72
Bailly, Alexis, fur trader, 14
Baker, Benjamin F., trader, 21
Baker's Settlement, 21, 22
Balloon, Zeppelin's flight in, 26
Banfield Island, 38
Banking, first bank in St. Anthony, 51; chain banking, 69. *See also* Finance.
Baptists, 36, 61
Bassett's Creek, 57
Bean, Reuben, 32, 42
Beltrami, Giacomo, 17
Benson, Lyman L., 37
Bernhardt, Sara, 59
Bliss, Major John, 19
Blue Earth Reservation, 40
Boom Island, 32
Bottineau, Pierre, trader, 29, 32
Bradley, Miles A., banker, 51

Bremer, Fredrika, novelist, 61
Bridal Veil Falls, 37
Bridge Square, 47, 53, 57, 72
Bridges, 41, 53
British, fur trading in U. S., 9, 11; agitation among Indians, 22
Buffalo, New York, 70
Building construction, boom 48; after fire, 59; 1927, 71
Bull, Ole, violinist, 51
Burroughs, Ira, 30
Business Directory, 38

Calhoun Beach Club, 71
Camp Coldwater, 12, 21
Cantonment New Hope, 12, 14, 17
Carpenter, Sergeant Nathaniel, 28
Carver, Jonathan, explorer, 9, 27
Cass, Governor Lewis, of Wisconsin, 13
Cataract House, 53
Catholics, 35
Catlin, George, artist, 20
Census dispute, 67
Center Block, 37
Chalybeate Springs, 51
Chambers, Thomas, 47
Cheever House, 37
Cheever, William A., 37
Chief Mahgossau, 13
Chippewa (Ojibway) Indians, warfare with Sioux, 16; games, 20; need for mission, 24
Christmas, at Fort Snelling, 18
Churches, First Presbyterian, 20; Protestant, 35; festivals, 36. *see also* Catholics
City Council, 51
City government, forms of, 51; two maintained, 58
City Hall, 63
Civil War, 21, 62; troops at Fort Snelling, 25, 27; volunteers in Minneapolis, 53; encourages flour milling, 57
Claim jumpers, 45, 48
Clark, Charlotte O., 15
Clark, Malcolm, 15
Clark, Nathan, 13
Clayton County, Iowa, 23
Cleveland, Mrs. Grover, 65
Congregational Church, 52
Conner, E. H., 41
Cooke, Jay, financier, 62
Cruttenden, Joel, 34
Cummings, Robert W., 30
Cushing, Caleb, 30

[89]

Daily Minnesotian, newspaper, 50
Dakota Territory, 55
Danz Orchestra, 73
David Copperfield, novel, 35
Depew, Chauncey, 66
Desnoyer, Stephen, 37
Donnelly, Ignatius, 26
Dugas, William, 30, 32

Eastman, Captain Seth, 24
Eastman, Rollins and Upton, 57
Eatonville, 19
Education, at Fort Snelling, 14; Sunday School at Fort Snelling, 15; Chaplain Gear as schoolmaster, 24; in St. Anthony, 33; in Minneapolis, 46, 49; school for immigrants, 61; Board of Education, 74. see also University of Minnesota
Emerson, John, surgeon, 21
Equal Right and Impartial Protection Claim Association, 46, 48
Eustis, Mayor W. H., 67

Fairs, 47, 61
Falls City, steamboat, 38
Falls, of St. Anthony. See St. Anthony Falls
Ferry, 32, 40
Finance, script issued, 50; first bank in St. Anthony, 51; Financial development of Minneapolis, 68; statistics, 69; crisis, 72
Findley, Samuel J., 29
Fires, schoolhouse burned, 49; need for firefighting equipment, 58; mill disaster, 63
First Methodist Episcopal Church, 36, 40
First Minnesota Regiment, 25
First Presbyterian Church of Minneapolis, 20
Fisher, Jacob, 30
Fletcher, Dr. Hezekiah, 45, 47
Flour Milling, first attempt, 15; government grist mill, 29, 42; in St. Anthony, 40, 56; effect of coopers' strike, 60; after mill disaster, 63; captures world market, 64; suffers from I.C.C. ruling, 70
Floyd, John B., Secretary of War, 25
Folsom, Edgar, 32
Folsom, S. P., 33
Forsyth, Major Thomas, 11
Fort St. Anthony, cornerstone laid, 13; description of, 15, *see also* Fort Snelling
Fort Snelling named, 16; social life at, 18; dramatics, 21; squatters expelled, 22; importance declines, 25; troops at during Civil War, 25, 27; corrupt influences in sale of public lands, 42, 45; city planned on site, 50
Foshay Tower, 71
Foshay, Wilbur, 72
Fourth of July, at Fort Snelling, 20
Freight rates, 70
French, attitude toward colonization, 9; inhabitants, 19; squatters, 29
Fur trade, 9. See also American Fur Company, Indian trade.

Garrioch, Peter, 21
Gear, Rev. Ezekiel Gilbert, 23, 35
Godfrey, Ard, millwright, 30, 32, 52; appointed as postmaster, 33; settles west of river, 47
Godfrey, Harriet Razada, 33
Goodhue, James M., editor, 44
Gooding, Amelia, 14
Gorman, Governor Willis A., 48
Governor Ramsey, steamboat, 38
Greeley, Horace, editor, 55
Green, Lieutenant Platt Rogers, 14
Griffith, T. J., engineer, 41
Groseilliers, Medard Chouart, sieur de, 9

Hamilton, Mrs. Elizabeth S., 22
Hamilton, James W., 15
Harmon, Allen, 45
Harrison's Hall, 59
Hastings, 55
Hennepin Avenue, 46, 49, 53
Hennepin County, organized, 46; issues script, 50
Hennepin County Agricultural Society, 47
Hennepin, Father Louis, passes site of Fort Snelling, 9; proposal to name Minneapolis after, 46
Hennepin Island, 31, 57
Henry M. Rice, steamboat, 38
Hindoo, steamboat, 38
Hoag, Ada, 46
Hoag, Charles, 46
Hole-In-The-Day, Chippewa chief, 31
Holidays, attitude towards, 38; *see also* specific holidays
Horse racing, 61
Hotchkiss, William A., editor, 49
Hotels, 34, 37, 38, 49, 51, 53, 65

Immigration, type of, 33, 39; after panic of 1857, 50; increase after Civil War, 55; Scandinavians, 61
Indian Lands, claim extinguished, 29; title to timber, 31

[90]

Indians, French influence among, 9; tribal differences, 16; agricultural colonies, 19; whiskey sold to, 22, 24; American Fur Company, 23; worship St. Anthony Falls, 28; settlers' attitude toward, 40; Sioux uprising, 54; *see also* Sioux, Chippewa
Industrial development, retarded, 48; diversification of, 71
Industrial Exposition Building, 65
Industry, Minneapolis' claim to industrial leadership, 58
Irving, Sir Henry, 59
Interstate Commerce Commission, 70

Jackins, John, 45, 47
"Jay Gould's Banana Belt," Northern Pacific Railroad, 64
Jefferson, Barracks, 18
Jobbing and wholesaling, 68
Johnson, Lieutenant R. W., 35

Kansas City, Missouri, 70
Kaposia, 19
Kegan Lake, 65
Kemper, Bishop Jackson, 24
King, William S., 61

LaCrosse, game, 20
Labor, need of laborers, 39; wages decline, 49; lack of during Civil War, 53; lumberjacks, 56; strike, 60; first union organized, 66; Minneapolis as market for, 68; unemployment, 71; truck drivers' strike, 72
La Croix, Edmund N., 64
Lady Franklin, steamboat, 38
Lagrue, *voyageur*, 29
Lake Amelia (Nokomis), 24
Lake Calhoun, 19, 44
Lake Harriet, 21, 70
Lake Minnetonka, 51, 70
Lake Nokomis, *see* Lake Amelia
Lake of the Isles, 70
Lamartine, steamboat, 37
Land rush, 45
Landry, Charles, *voyageur*, 29.
Latin America, 72
Law enforcement, 23; hanging of leaders of Sioux uprising, 26; need for jail, 58
Lawyers, 59
Le Sueur, Pierre Charles, at the Minnesota river, 9
Leavenworth, Colonel Henry, expedition to establish fort, 12; clashes with Taliaferro, 13

Lennon, John G., 34
Lewis, David, weaver, 57
Liberal League, 59
Libraries, *see* Public libraries; St. Anthony Library Association
Liquor trade, 22, 39; *see also* Temperance
Livestock, importation of, 44; in streets of Minneapolis, 59
Long, Major Stephen H., exploration and report, 11; expedition to Red River, 17
Loomis, Colonel Gustavus, 20, 24
Loring and Fletcher, 63
Louisiana Purchase, 9
Lowry, Thomas, financier, 62, 66
Lumber, scarcity of milled, 32; amount of timber supply, 30; workers in, 49; as medium of exchange, 50
Lumbering, 28; eastern capital for, 30, 34; government mill, 14, 31; growth in production, 40; rise of, in Minneapolis, 56; decline, 67

Macalester College, 65
Mansfield, Richard, 59
Manufacturing, 73
Marryat, Captain Frederick, writer, 22
Marsh, John, teacher, 14
Marshall, Joseph, 34
Marshall, William R., 32; opens store, 34; in territorial legislature, 34; first survey of Minneapolis townsite, 47
Martin Chuzzlewit, novel, 35
McDonald, John, 30
McKinley, William, 65
McLean, C. W., 52
Medicine, 45; practice of, 24, 33
Medicine Bottle, Sioux Indian, 26
Menck, Henry C., 23
Mendota, 12, 17
Merchandising, 36, 47; first store, St. Anthony, 31, 34; merchants reluctant to accept script, 50
Middlings purifier, milling process, 64
Military, discipline, 18, 19, 22; obstacle against settlement, 42, 47; *see also* Fort Snelling, Civil War
Mill disaster, 63
Miller, Mary E., 46
Minneapolis, 41, 44; naming of, 46; as vacation center, 51; industrial center, 55; flour milling at, 57; absorbs St. Anthony, 58, 61; town government organized, 51; result of uniting cities, 66; financial center, 69; cultural position, 73
Minneapolis Board of Education, 74
Minneapolis Bridge Company, 41

[91]

Minneapolis Chamber of Commerce, 64
Minneapolis Institute of Art, 74
Minneapolis Symphony Orchestra, 73
Minnehaha Creek, 24, 47
Minnehaha Falls, 51, 62
Minnesota and Pacific Railroad, 54
Minnesota Arts Council, 74
Minnesota Central Railroad, 55
Minnesota City, 50
Minnesota Mill, 57
Minnesota Pioneer, newspaper, 36, 44
Minnesota River, 9, 50
Minnesota Territory, organization of, 24; struggle over location of capital, 34; number of farms in, 1850, 44
Minnetonka Mills, 63
Missionaries, 20, 24
Mississippi River, 9, 28, 50; ferry across, 32; dispute over head of navigation, 37; see also Steamboat transportation
Missouri Compromise, 21
Mitropoulous, Dimitri, 73
Monsier Tonson, drama, 21
Mousseaux, Charles, 44
Municipal Auditorium, 71
Muscatine, Iowa, 44
Music, 51, 73

Neill, Rev. Edward D., 35
New England, immigrants from, 33, 35; cultural influence of, 35, 59; standard of comparison, 47, 58, 61; moral standards applied to Minneapolis, 58
Newspapers, first newspaper in St. Anthony, 39; St. Paul's attitude towards St. Anthony, 44; first in Minneapolis, 49; comment on industrial development, 55; stir up Twin City rivalry, 661; see specific newspapers
Nicolet, Jean, explorer, 9
Nicollet Avenue, 70
Nicollet House, 49
Nicollet Island, 31, 35
Nicollet, Joseph Nicolas, explorer, 20
Ninth Federal Reserve District, 69
North, John W., 35, 52
Northern Pacific Railway, 64
Northern Star, steamboat, 38
Northfield, village, 58
Northup, Anson, 34, 46
Northwestern Democrat, newspaper, 49
Northwestern Telephone Company, 63
Norwegians, 61
Nyberg, Nils, 61

Oberhoffer, Emil, 73

Old Main Hall, 53
Ormandy, Eugene, 73

Palmyra, steamboat, 29
Panama Canal, 70
Panic, of 1857, 49; of 1873, 62; of 1893, 67; of 1929, 71
Patch, Luther, 30, 31
Patch, Marion, 31
Patti, Adelina, 51
Pembina, 17
Pence Opera House, 59
Philharmonix Orchestra, 73
Pierce, Thomas W., 48
Pike, Lieutenant, Zebulon M., expedition to Minnesota, 10; his treaty with the Sioux ratified, 11
Pike Rapids, 30
Pike's Island, 10
Pond, Gideon, 19, 44
Pond, Samuel, 19, 44
Population, of Fort Snelling reserve, 22; garrisoned at Fort, 1849, 24; of St. Anthony, 29, 33; census dispute between Minneapolis and St. Paul, 66
Powers, Simon, 36
Plympton, Major Joseph, 22, 28
Postal service, 14; first postoffice, St. Anthony, 33; at Fort Snelling, 43; at Minneapolis, 47
Prairie du Chien, Wis., 12, 14, 16, 17
Prescott, Philander, interpreter, 44
Prize fights, 65
Protestant Episcopal Church, 24
Public lands, efforts to secure, 42, 43; sale of, 32, 47; claims on, 45
Public Library, first in state, 35; Minneapolis Public Library, 53; interesting securing, 59

Quarrying, first in Minnesota, 14
Quinn, Peter, 29

Radisson, Pierre d'Esprit, explorer, 9
Railroad, opened to La Crosse, 51; between St. Anthony and St. Paul, 54; northwest route to Pacific, 64
Ramsey County, 24, 48
Ramsey, Governor Alexander, 37, 38
Rantoul, Robert, 30
Reachi, Joseph, *voyageur*, 29
Real estate, boom in, 48; deflation of, 49; speculative madness, 56
Red River, flood in 1826, 14; Long expedition to, 17; — carts, 17, 21; — trade, 36

[92]

Red Wing, village, 55
Religion, first Protestant church in Upper Mississippi Valley, 20; first resident pastor of white community, 24; desire for churches, St. Anthony, 35; *see also* Missionaries, specific churches
Republican National Convention, 1892, 65
Reserve Bank Organization Committee, 69
River navigation, above St. Anthony Falls, 29, 38; above St. Paul, 36; rafting of lumber, 56; modern river transportation, 72; *see also* Steamboat transportation
River St. Pierre, *see* Minnesota River
Rogers, R. C., 40
Rollins, Captain John, 34, 38
Rum River, 30
Russell, Lillian, 59
Russell, Roswell P., merchant, 31, 34

St. Anthony, village, description of, 1848, 30; type of settlers, 33; ambition to become capital, 34; social life in, 35, 38; as head of navigation, 37; first newspaper in, 39; opening of suspension bridge, 41; interest in town across the river, 44; made part of Hennepin County, 49; issues script, 1857, 50; united with Minneapolis, 58, 61
St. Anthony City, Cheevertown, 37
St. Anthony Express, newspaper, 39, 46, 47
St. Anthony Falls, included in Pike's treaty, 10; sawmill built at, 14; grist mill at, 15, 29; sale of water power rights, 30; Greeley's opinion of, 55; collapse of, 60
St. Anthony Library Association, 35
St. Anthony Republican, newspaper, 52
St. Charles Hotel, 34, 38
St. Cloud, 38
St. Croix River, 10, 29
St. Louis, 10, 18, 56, 57
St. Paul, 27, 35, 40, 44, 48, 50; early reputation, 24; opposition to its being capital, 34; as a merchant city, 36; attitude toward St. Anthony, 41; railroad between St. Paul and St. Anthony, 54; maintains trade leadership in 1860's, 55; rivalry with Minneapolis, 66
St. Paul and Pacific Railway, 54
St. Paul Gas Company, 26
St. Peter, 55
St. Peter's River, 10
see Minnesota River
Sallie St. Claire Troupe, 50
Sauk Rapids, 38
Saw mills, 14, 32, 34, 40, 47, 56; last Minneapolis mill closes, 67

Scofield, Mary A., 46
Scott, Captain Martin, 28
Scott, Dred, 21
Scott, General Winfield, 16
Secombe, Rev. Charles, 52
Selkirk Colony, refugees from, 14, 24, 42
Shakopee, Sioux chieftain, 26
Sibley, Henry Hastings, 17
Sioux (Dakota) Indians, 22, 25; Pike treaty with, 10; Sioux-Chippewa warfare, 16; feeling against whites, 17; agricultural colony, 19; mission at Lake Harriet, 21; treaties of 1851, 24; *see also* Indian trade, Sioux uprising
Sioux uprising, hanging of leaders, 26; refugees in Minneapolis, 54
Slavery, in Minneapolis, 51, 52
Smith, Congressman Robert, 42
Snelling, Elizabeth, 14
Snelling, Colonel Josiah, arrives at Fort, 13; appointment to Jefferson Barracks, 18; character of, 18; proposal to name county after, 46
Snelling, William Joseph, 15, 18
Southern, tourists in Minneapolis, 51; trade halted by war, 54
Speculators, 47, 49
Spirit Island, 38
Stagecoach lines, forerunners of, 34; between St. Anthony and St. Paul, 36; stations, 37
Stanchfield, Daniel, 30, 31, 34
Steamboat construction, 38
Steamboat transportation, 18, 19, 22, 29; first in Upper Mississippi, 15; hazards above St. Paul, 36; efforts to reach St. Anthony, 37; to St. Anthony, 38; halted by Civil War, 54
Steele, Franklin, sutler at Fort Snelling, 22; purchase of Fort reserve, 25, 50; rental for reserve, 26; claim on St. Anthony Falls, 28; seeks eastern capital, 30, 31; sells half interest in holdings, 34; influence of, 43, 45
Stephens, Rev. Enos, 36
Stevens, Rev. Jedediah D., 20, 21
Stevens, John H., arrival of, 42; farm in Minneapolis, 44
Stevens, Mary, 44
Stillwater, 55
Stone, Frank, 52
Street railways, 62
Streets, description of, 53, 62
Swan River, 30
Swedish immigration, 61

[93]

Taliaferro, Lieutenant Lawrence, arrives at Fort Snelling, 13; relations with Indians, 18; establishes Indian colony, 19; resignation of, 23
Talcott, Orlando, 49
Tapper, Captain John, 30
Taverns, 37
Taylor, Arnold W., 34
Taylor, Zachary, 23
Telegraph, 54
Telephone, 62
Temperance, community attitude, 39; organization, 48
Tenth Avenue Bridge, 37
Territorial Legislature, 34
Terry, Ellen, 59
Textiles, 46, 55, 57
Thanksgiving, 38
Theatre, at Fort Snelling, 21; first in Minneapolis, 50; hall with stage equipment, 59
Trade Unions, 60, 66, 72
Traffic problems, 59
Transportation, need for, 36
see also Steamboat transportation, Railroads, Stagecoach lines, River navigation
Tully, Andrew, 15
Tully, John, 15
Tuttle, Calvin, 30
Twin City rivalry, 55, 66

Universalists, 36, 37, 53, 74
University of Minnesota, awarded to St. Anthony, 34, 74

Verrall, John, composer, 73

Verbrugghen, Henri, 73
Village Lawyer, The, drama, 21
Villard, Henry, 64
Virginia, steamboat, 15

Walker Art Center, 74
Walker, T. B., 73
Washington Avenue, 49, 53
War of 1812, 11
Washburn "A" Mill, 63
Welles, H. T., 51
West Hotel, 65
Westphal Brewery, 65
Whiskey, 43, *see also* Liquor trade
White Buzzard, *see* Chief Mahgossau
"Wildcat paper," money, 50; *see also* Finance
William Crooks, locomotive, 54
Williams, Thomas Hale, 53
Williamson, Rev. Thomas S., 20
Willoughby, Amherst, 36
Winnebago Indians, 40
Winona, 55
Winslow House, 51, 54, 65
Winslow, James M., 51
Winston, Eliza, 52
Wood Lake, 54
Woodman's Hall, 50
Woodman, Ivory T., 50
Work Projects Administration, 72, 74
World War, 70

Yellowstone Expedition, 13

Zeppelin, Count von, 26